CRADLE

—— OF THE ——

TEXAS

REPUBLIC

CRADLE

OF THE

TEXAS

REPUBLIC

DR. ROBIN MONTGOMERY AND JOY MONTGOMERY

THE
History
PRESS

Published by The History Press
Charleston, SC
www.historypress.com

Cover images courtesy of Library of Congress.

First published 2022

Manufactured in the United States

ISBN 9781467151900

Library of Congress Control Number: 2022930163

CONTENTS

CONTENTS

PREFACE

*C*radle of the Texas Republic is a feature of a task force on our Cradle area addressing multiple aspects of interest. Given that the task force addresses items within the confines of the original Montgomery County area, it is sometimes referenced as the "Montgomery County Taskforce." Originally the vision of Joy Montgomery, the task force concept centers on the pivotal role of historical interpretation of the temper of our times.

Other task force projects underway, as this book goes to press, include the following:

1. A study of African American freedom communities and cemeteries, including accompanying genealogical studies. Working on this study are Ann Meador, chair, Annette Kerr, Cindy Cheney, Dr. Marilyn Byrd and Cynthia Stubblefield Walker.

2. A study of the routes of ancient trails and traces under the guidance of Darrell Hebert, utilizing, where possible, lidar technology.

3. A musical album featuring original songs about our region. Pursuing this project are Robin Montgomery, Mary McCoy, Jimmy Montgomery, Ann Meador and Joy Montgomery.

4. A cultural paradigm of our region is under production by Stormy Montgomery, Cathy Holden, Joy Montgomery and Rosanna Roxi Montgomery.

5. Historical tours of the Cradle of Texas Road and between that road and such objectives as Maryville, Tennessee, boyhood home of Sam Houston, under the general direction of Joy and Robin Montgomery.

The task force welcomes further ideas and participation.

ACKNOWLEDGEMENTS

This book is dedicated to the Henderson Yoakum Chapter of the Sons of the Republic of Texas, along with Luke and Stormy Montgomery. Also, a special thanks to the Montgomery Texas Historical Society, the Lone Star Chapter of the Sons of the Republic of Texas, Joe Kolb and the Heritage Museum of Montgomery County and to the Montgomery and Walker County Historical Commissions.

Additionally, with deep gratitude to Zoe Ames, Ben Gibson and the staff of The History Press for accommodating and time-sensitive support.

PREAMBLE AND THEME

Our Cradle of Texas region, bounded by the Brazos to the Trinity Rivers, west to east, and Spring Creek to the Old San Antonio Road, south to north, constituted a huge area of Texas before and during the era of the Texas Republic of 1836–46. Formed as Montgomery County on December 14, 1837, during the republic era, that county contained all or part of six present counties, with the town of Montgomery named the county seat in 1838. Walker and Grimes Counties broke off first, in 1846, as statehood began. We've also tangentially added Washington on the Brazos to our Cradle region, for the area of original Montgomery County was included in that region at the time of the Texas Constitutional Convention as part of Washington Municipality.

As will be shown, the history of this region includes an endemic link to even further territory west of the Brazos. Central to our theme is the historical conditioning of the value base of this vast area as a motivating force for unity, both within our area and as a model for the larger breadth of the United States, where regions could seek common ground in their area history.

The values of the Texas Republic, and hence of our region, link directly to the foundational documents of the United States. Evidence lies in the mindset reflected in the reasons given for independence from Mexico in the Texas Declaration of Independence on March 2, 1836, a declaration written the night before at Groce's Retreat across the Brazos in the area of our Cradle of Texas Road:

The Mexican government, by its colonization laws, invited and induced the Anglo-American population of Texas to colonize its wilderness under the pledged faith of a written constitution, that they should continue to enjoy the constitutional liberty and republican government to which they had been habituated in the land of their birth, the United States of America.

The Father of Texas, Stephen F. Austin, expressed similar sentiments in his letter to Andrew Jackson seeking Jackson's support for a Texas revolution:

This people look to you as the guardians of their rights and privileges.... Are we not, the Texians, obeying the dictates of an education received here: from you the American people, from your fathers, from the patriots of '76— the Republicans of 1836?

The Austin quote links the budding Texas Republic directly to the U.S. Declaration of Independence of July 4, 1776. Furthermore, the interchangeable terms "Anglo-Texian" and "Anglo-Texan" reinforce the identity with the parent U.S. Anglo-based culture. The preamble to the U.S. Declaration of Independence depicts the common cultural framework:

When in the course of Human Events it becomes necessary for one People to dissolve the Political Bands which connected them with another, and to assume the separate and equal station to which the Laws of Nature and Nature's God entitle them, a decent respect to the opinions of Mankind requires that they should declare the causes which impel them to Separation.

We hold these Truths to be self-evident, that all Men are Created equal, that they are endowed by their Creator with certain unalienable Rights, that among these are Life, Liberty and the Pursuit of Happiness. That to secure these Rights, Governments are instituted among Men, drawing their just Powers from the Consent of the Governed.

It is around this theme that we build our goal of forging a basis for unity applicable to all regions of the United States, a unity formed in a realistic appraisal of the goals of our common founders.

As this work is written, the United States is in the throes of a cultural battle centered on its legacy of slavery. Like the parent United States, the Texas Republic condoned this awful practice. Yet, linked explicitly to the U.S. Declaration of Independence, the former slaves and former slave masters can join hands in celebration of their common heritage as reflected in the Civil Rights Acts of 1964 and 1965.

We thus are seeking a realistic assessment of our common history through studying each era in terms of its own propensities and perspectives in the long drive for equality. All of us inherit a legacy replete with both conflict and resolution. A realistic appraisal of our past will address all aspects with reason and understanding of the mindset distinct to each of the evolving eras of our history, in recognition of the frailty of human nature inherent in us all.

Here again, we draw upon the legacy of the Texas Republic, in this case in the words of John O'Sullivan, who coined the term "Manifest Destiny" during the convergence process of the Texas Republic into the State of Texas in late 1845:

> *The Independence of Texas was complete and absolute. It was an independence, not only in fact, but of right…all that without agency of government—in the national flow of events, the spontaneous working of principles.*

Kenneth Anderson gravesite in Anderson, Texas, across the street from the Fanthorp Inn. *Courtesy of Robin Montgomery.*

Here O'Sullivan was drawing upon a mindset reflected in an earlier article of his, dating to 1839, depicting the nature of the United States itself. Instead of remaining eternally living in a divided past conditioned by slavery, he states:

> *Our national birth was the beginning of a new history, the formation and progress of an untried political system, which separates us from the past and connects with the future only.... The US government was different than any nation, it would have to create its own destiny.*

O'Sullivan coined his term Manifest Destiny in 1845, even as Kenneth Lewis Anderson, last vice president of Texas, en route to his home in East Texas, died in what became known as Anderson due to this event. Significantly, he had just presided over official actions setting the stage for Texas to become a state.

In summary, then, we seek to promote an approach to history centered on, we think, a realistic appraisal of human nature, centered in the thinking behind the U.S. Declaration of Independence, holding humanity as imperfect by nature but capable of redemption through a future-based focus centering on friendship, reflection and, most of all, forgiveness and equality. These tasks, we believe, constitute the best course toward unity on all levels.

Our Two-Part Approach

This work is divided into two separate but interrelated parts. Part I consists of an introduction to our Cradle area and concept, followed by a general history of the region since ancient times, with emphasis on how it addressed the Texas Revolution and republic era. Included are many personalities and stories. Part II will center on how the spirit of Manifest Destiny found expression in our history.

Our objectives include:

1. Promoting discussion groups via presentations to civic organizations, churches and public and private schools
2. Occasional general assemblies of principals of the various sites and cities in our region to share ideas and seek motivation

3. Publication of pamphlets, documentaries, musical albums and dramas
4. Promoting various sites, associations and ideas of the present in our area
5. Looking toward making our area an official historic Texas Trail

It is our hope that each of our readers will address these objectives in light of his or her respective talents and conditions. Whether young or old, each will seek to ferret out incidents and sites in our respective areas that can enhance our common regional story, sparking unity and inspiration to us all. From gatherings of friends, to use of the telephone, to making presentations, together we can make the Cradle of Texas area a clarion call to fulfillment of the American Dream, from the regional to the national level.

CHAPTER 1

THE CRADLE OF TEXAS ROAD

AN INTRODUCTION

I n 2013, we published a book entitled *The Cradle of Texas Road: A Model of Cultural Integration for the Nation.* Our envisioned road—the Cradle region—coincided with the boundaries of the original Montgomery County plus Washington-on-the-Brazos. The timing of the publication date centered on a Texas Legacy Fest that we, along with Rita Wiltz, Theresa Thornhill and Maria Baños Jordan, were promoting in Conroe, celebrating the 200th anniversary of the first attempt to establish an independent Republic of Texas in 1813. The first formal declaration of that then-impending republic occurred in the vicinity of the northeastern sector of our proposed Cradle Road.

Our four-part, two-day Legacy Fest featured representatives from each of the cardinal points along the proposed Cradle of Texas Road. The representatives each discussed their location and its potential significance to the concept of a formal road for tourist travel and historical research.

We are engaged in research linked to that 2013 Legacy Fest, with the intention to consummate the declaration made there to formalize the concept of the Cradle of Texas Road as a Texas "Road of Interest."

Toward this purpose, we will begin with an overview of a few of the key points of historical interest extant in the sites linked to the Cradle project, then proceed to chapters with reference both to the road and to the general history of the area.

MONTGOMERY

We begin in Montgomery, the county seat of our Cradle of Texas Road during most of the era of the Texas Republic.

HOMESITE AND GRAVE OF CHARLES STEWART. Charles Stewart was Texas's first secretary of state and the officially recognized designer of the Texas Lone Star Flag. The site is near the intersection of Highway 105 and FM 2824.

NAT HART DAVIS MUSEUM. City and county museum off Main Street, named for an early district judge.

A historical marker is here, featuring one of the extant opinions as to who named Montgomery: in this case, W.W. Shepperd, naming it for Lemuel Montgomery.

DOBBIN

A few miles below Dobbin is a marker for the Noah Griffith Home, associated with the "Babe of the Alamo," Angelina Dickinson, who married Noah's son, John Meynard Griffith.

JACOB SHANNON EVERGREEN CEMETERY

Just west of Dobbin and to the north off Highway 105 is a historic cemetery named for Jacob Shannon, early pioneer of Montgomery County, whose homesite was just north of the cemetery. Featured among the gravesites is that of Margaret Montgomery Shannon. She was the wife of Owen Shannon. The couple were among the early residents of Montgomery, and Margaret is another of the possibilities considered as the namesake of the town and county of Montgomery.

PLANTERSVILLE

Plantersville is located off Highways 105 and 1774, at the juncture of three early land grants, received by Asa Yeamon, John Landrum and William Montgomery.

JOEL GREENWOOD CEMETERY. This cemetery is four miles north and to the west of 1774, with key personalities of early Montgomery County history buried there, including probably Owen Shannon, husband of Margaret Montgomery. James and William Montgomery are two other possible candidates for the namesake of Montgomery and Montgomery County.

GRAVE OF J.G.W. PIERSON. Pierson occupied several key positions in Pecan Point off Red River in the early 1820s, including sheriff. He was also interim director of Robertson's Colony in Texas as well as a member of the Consultation and head of the Washington County Militia in 1836. Also buried here is Elizabeth Montgomery, second wife of Pierson.

HIGH POINT AND STONEHAM

HIGH POINT. A community west of Plantersville, founded by J.G.W. Pierson.

STONEHAM CEMETERY. Started by Franklin Greenwood; includes the graves of Andrew and John Montgomery, brothers who fought together at the Battle of San Jacinto and worked with Pierson in Robertson's Colony. There is an official Texas historical marker in the cemetery for Andrew Montgomery, as namesake for the town and county of Montgomery.

GRIMES PRAIRIE

Just north of Highway 105 past the Stoneham Cemetery, Grimes Prairie was the home of Jesse Grimes, the first chief justice of Montgomery County and president *pro tempore* of the Republic of Texas senate. In the District of Viesca, Grimes was a surveyor, head of militia and *syndico procurador*. While attending the Constitutional Convention at Washington-on-the-Brazos in March 1836, he received perhaps the last letter of William B. Travis from the Alamo. He also ran for lieutenant governor, allied to Sam Houston, in 1857.

NAVASOTA

LA SALLE STATUES. One statue is on Washington Avenue in the middle of the street. The other is in the flag park west of town near the VFW Hall. René-

Statue of La Salle in western Navasota, off the road to Washington-on-the-Brazos, behind the flag park across from the VFW Hall. *Courtesy of Robin Montgomery.*

Robert Cavelier, Sieur de La Salle, constitutes the basis for the naming of the Cradle of Texas Road, as his presence prompted the move to construct San Francisco de las Tejas, the mission associated with the naming of Texas (see Chapter 2).

LA BAHIA TRAIL. Historical marker off La Salle Street depicting the historic trail from La Bahia to the San Antonio Road.

FRANK HAMMER STATUE. On the courthouse lawn, a Russell Cushman–built statue depicts Hammer as marshal of Navasota. He later directed the demise of Bonnie and Clyde.

MANCE LIPSCOMB STATUE. Off La Salle Street. Lipscomb was a high-time blues singer.

ANDERSON

Ten miles east of Navasota off Highway 90. Its most distinctive historical markers include the Fanthorp Inn and the gravesite of the last vice president of the Texas Republic, Kenneth Lewis Anderson.

Fanthorp Inn and Stage Stop. *Courtesy of Wikipedia.*

ROANS PRAIRIE

Located at the intersection of Highways 90 and 30.

HOME OF JOSHUA HADLEY. Hadley was the alcalde of Washington Municipality.

SHIRO

The town is four miles east of Roans Prairie on Highway 30.

ABRAHAM ZUBER HOME. The home was about one mile south of Shiro off 1486. It was the site to which Moses Rose came from the Alamo, after being the only one failing to answer William B. Travis's call to "cross this line should you wish to stay, before Santa Anna attacks the Alamo."

ZUBER MUSEUM: Western fringe of Shiro and south of 105.

BEDIAS

A town north of Roans Prairie off Highway 90. Named for the Bidai (or Bedias) Indians. A Bidai trail came through the area. North of Bedias is the gravesite of Sarah Dodson, famous for her Lone Star Flag design.

Sarah Dodson grave, north of Bedias in Bethel Cemetery. She fashioned a Lone Star flag for her husband's company that flew in several engagements of the Texas Revolution and is an official symbol of Grimes County. *Courtesy of Robin Montgomery.*

MADISONVILLE

Off Highways 90 and 21. Near to Midway, where nearby there is a marker to Trinidad, a former community with links to the First Republic of Texas via the Magee-Gutiérrez Expedition in 1812–13.

HUNTSVILLE

South of Madisonville off Interstate 45, including the following sites:

SAM HOUSTON MEMORIAL MUSEUM AND PARK. Features two Sam Houston homes.

SAM HOUSTON'S GRAVE.

SAM HOUSTON STATUE VISITOR CENTER.

THE GIBBS-POWELL HOUSE. Also known as the WALKER COUNTY MUSEUM.

PLEASANT GRAY SITE. Off downtown square. Gray was the founder of Huntsville.

THE TEXAS STATE PENITENTIARY "WALLS UNIT." Opened in 1849.

WILLIS

Twenty or so miles south of Huntsville off Interstate 45.

Tobacco from Willis received first prize at the World's Columbian Exhibition in Chicago in 1893 and Paris, France, in 1900. Once eight cigar factories were there.

Near Willis off old Highway 75 is a marker to General Richard Montgomery of Revolutionary War fame, killed at Quebec and another possibility for the namesake of the county.

CONROE

Home of the Heritage Museum of Montgomery County. At the time of this writing, the fastest-growing community in the United States, in one of the fastest-growing counties; the heartbeat of Conroe is attuned to Texas culture.

THE LONE STAR MONUMENT AND HISTORICAL FLAG PARK. The flag park is the vision of Craig Campobella and entails thirteen of the flags of the revolutionary era of Texas history. Inside the semicircle of flags stands a magnificent statue by Campobella entitled *The Texian*. A poem to the statue is

Conroe Flag Park scene. *Courtesy of the Flag Park Association.*

featured in stone nearby under the authorship of David Parsons of Conroe, a poet laureate of Texas. Also in the flag park is the Campobella statue of Charles Stewart, the first secretary of state and the officially recognized designer of the official Lone Star Flag of Texas.

MONTGOMERY COUNTY WALKWAY THROUGH TIME. This is a seventy-foot mural by Mark Clapham spanning Davis Street in downtown Conroe. The mural records key segments of Montgomery County history.

WASHINGTON-ON-THE-BRAZOS

Here, linked to our Cradle Road but west of the Brazos, is the site of the Constitutional Convention of March 1–17, 1836. At Independence Hall, the Texas Declaration of Independence and Constitution received birth, and Sam Houston received election as leader of both the regular and volunteer armies.

Independence Hall. *Courtesy of Joy Montgomery.*

PART I

GENERAL HISTORY AND OVERVIEW

CHAPTER 2

MONTGOMERY COUNTY

AN OVERVIEW

INTRODUCTION

Upon describing the political development of the original county, we will isolate key events in the area that impact larger Texas history, both before and after the birth of the county. These events begin with the exploits of René-Robert Cavelier, Sieur de La Salle, whose adventures affected multiple nations from the 1680s through present times, including the event that led to the naming of Texas itself, and an introduction to the history of the Bidai Indian tribe, original kingpin of Texas.

Then we address an event replete with adventure and lessons for our time in the first successful—but temporary—run to make Texas a state. This is typically referenced as the "Gutiérrez-Magee Expedition," which introduced the Alabama-Coushatta Indians. The Coushatta form a link to the second effort to form a Republic of Texas, the James Long Expedition of 1819–21.

Then we move to an introduction of Washington Municipality, within which the area of original Montgomery County once lay. A political leader of that municipality, Joshua Hadley, made his home in the area of original Montgomery County. As Washington Municipality evolved into Washington County, we introduce a most amazing man, J.G.W. Pierson, head of the Washington County Militia.

Pierson is then shown to link to others of the original Montgomery County: for example, via his role as interim director of the huge Robertson's Colony, charged with establishing what was projected to be the capital of all of Texas until it was overwhelmed by the worst Indian fighting in Texas history.

With Pierson, we also link to the era of Texas's independence struggles, bringing up the indomitable Sam Houston, leader of the forces of the Battle of San Jacinto. Here we address citizens of the original county who served in that great battle, plus a connection to William B. Travis drawing a line in the sand at the Alamo, asking all who chose to stay to cross. One didn't, and his story is recorded here.

Next we reach immediate events leading to the birth of the county, featuring the amazing Jesse Grimes, significant as a senator of the republic and as the first chief justice of the county. Included here will be the story of the choice of Montgomery as the county seat.

From this point, we dwell on events in the county that reference the era of the larger Republic of Texas, within which the original county lay.

ORIGINAL MONTGOMERY COUNTY

Roots of Montgomery County reach to the independence of Mexico from Spain in 1821. By 1824, Mexican Texas allied with the state of Coahuila, the capital of which was in Saltillo. From 1824 until 1831, Texas consisted of one department, headquartered in San Antonio. In 1831 the Department of Nacogdoches was added, while 1834 witnessed the birth of the Department of the Brazos, with its capital at San Felipe de Austin.

The Department of the Brazos stretched west to east from the Lavaca River to the watershed between the San Jacinto and Trinity Rivers and south to north from the Gulf to the Red River. By the time of the Independence Convention at Washington-on-the-Brazos in March 1836, stretched over the three departments were twenty-three municipalities, entities similar to Anglo counties. Indeed, at that convention, on March 17, the Texans designated all twenty-three municipalities as counties.

One of the municipalities in the Department of the Brazos, established earlier in 1828, was Austin Municipality. Originally that municipality reached from the Lavaca to the San Jacinto River west to east while ranging from the Gulf to the San Antonio Road south to north. By 1833, Austin Municipality had expanded, incorporating such communities as Bastrop, Matagorda and Harrisburg.

Austin Municipality eventually broke up into fifteen smaller municipalities. One of these, formed in 1835, was Washington Municipality, headquartered at Washington-on-the-Brazos. When the Constitutional Convention declared all municipalities as counties, Washington Municipality became Washington County, occupying both sides of the Brazos River. Then began the breakup of this great county. On the west, the county yielded land for the new counties of Brazos, Washington, Burleson and Lee.

Meanwhile, settlers on the east side of the Brazos were frustrated with traveling the distance to Washington for official county business in an atmosphere of mosquitoes. Consequently, several petitions from the settlers led, on December 14, 1837, to the birth of the new county of Montgomery. This was the third county, after Houston and Fannin, which the new Republic of Texas created.

The Texas legislature designated the borders of the new county to include "all that part of the County of Washington lying east of the Brazos, and southeast of the Navasota Rivers." This made clear the western border, while the northern border was clearly marked as the San Antonio Road. As heir of Washington Municipality, the southern border centered on Lake Creek. However, by 1840 it reached to Spring Creek.

The volatile search for an eastern border holds special interest to citizens of Conroe. On December 18, 1837, it was ruled that Liberty County would reach only nine miles west of the Trinity. Only then was it clear that the future Conroe and its immediate environs would rest exclusively within Montgomery County, for Liberty Municipality had stretched to the San Jacinto. Also, while part of the eastern boundary reached the Trinity, for a short time the area of future Conroe occupied an earlier version of Madison County, with a Hamilton County above and a Spring Creek County below, just above a bit of Harrisburg County.

To further complicate matters, three other colonial efforts centered on the San Jacinto as their western border. One of these was the aborted colony of Hayden Edwards, which lost its bearings in the ill-fated Fredonian Rebellion. Another was the colony of Joseph Vehlein, which fused into holdings of the Galveston Bay and Texas Land Company, headquartered in New York. The company's exotic and myriad machination meandered through and beyond the era of the Republic of Texas.

The third colonization effort whose legal jurisdiction spread westward to the San Jacinto was a colony in the Atascocita District. The colony was heir of a Spanish fort and military outpost established in the mid-eighteenth century to guard against French incursion into the area of the Trinity River. This area, called Liberty Municipality, stretched from the San Jacinto to the Sabine and from the Gulf to Nacogdoches. From 1826 to 1831, settlers from the United States exercised the authority of this vast Atascocita Mandate.

As things settled, in 1846, Grimes and Walker Counties were carved out of Montgomery County, to be followed in 1853 by a portion of later Madison County and in 1870 by a part of San Jacinto County. Finally, in 1873, Montgomery County gave way to a small section of Waller County.

Amazing are the crosscurrents of history that led to Montgomery County as we know it.

CHAPTER 3
GENESIS

LA SALLE AND THE BLUE NUN

The Frenchman René-Robert Cavelier, Sieur de La Salle, and María de Agreda, a nun of Spain, inadvertently generated conditions leading the Spanish to give the name of Texas to a substantial area north of the Rio Grande. La Salle sparked restlessness—the push—in the Spanish-controlled area called New Spain, while the saga of the Blue Nun marked the motivation—the pull—generating Spain's invitation to the place of the naming. In turn, La Salle's death near present Navasota fundamentally gave rise to the Cradle of Texas Road as a description of, essentially, the area of later original Montgomery County plus Washington-on-the-Brazos.

LA SALLE: THE PUSH

In 1682, La Salle, from his base in Canada, made his way to link the Mississippi River with the Gulf, claiming all land served by Mississippi tributaries for France while christening the area Louisiana for King Louis XIV of France and his wife, Anne. By this audacious act, he set in motion a tide of intrigue, which made an impact on the political culture of the North American continent hardly equaled in history. England and, later, its heir, the upstart United States, would both feel progressively more stifled, restless under their resultant confinement to the east of the Mississippi. More immediately, La Salle's proclamation motivated the Spanish—at the time sitting stunned in El Paso, licking their wounds in the wake of the Pueblo

RENE ROBERT CAVELIER
SIEUR DE LA SALLE

TREACHEROUSLY SLAIN BY HIS OWN
MEN NEAR THIS SPOT IN MARCH 1687

BORN ROUEN, FRANCE NOVEMBER 22, 1643
EXPLORER OF THE MISSISSIPPI RIVER
EXPLORER, STATESMAN, EMPIRE BUILDER
A NOBLEMAN IN RANK AND CHARACTER

ERECTED BY
THE TEXAS SOCIETY
OF THE DAUGHTERS OF THE
AMERICAN REVOLUTION AND
THE CITIZENS OF NAVASOTA
1936

La Salle statue, standing off Washington Avenue near midtown Navasota. *Courtesy of the Russell Cushman Collection.*

Revolt in New Mexico—to set their sights on occupying East Texas. This was a land prepared for a missionary thrust by the alleged astral projections to that area of a nun in Spain known to history as the "Blue Nun."

Along with the christening of Louisiana, La Salle placed a cross at the mouth of the great river, giving concrete substance to France's claim to a region covering the central portion of the whole later United States. He then hastened to France in late 1683 to present the good news to the king. With enthusiasm, the king endorsed La Salle's vision of a claim in the face of covetous eyes from New Spain in the west and Britain, later the United States, in the east. For La Salle personally, the outpost would serve to secure a foothold from which to establish a monopoly on the fur trade in the region.

As La Salle left Rochefort, France, on August 1, 1684, Spain and France were at war. Though the war ended soon after he sailed, La Salle was not privy to the news. Hence, he sailed into the Caribbean, a Spanish lake, prepared for an expected hostile reception. For instance, there were few females in his flotilla of four ships and only two families. The rest were males prepared for battle, should it be necessary.

Indeed, the prospects of hostility were not unfounded, for soon after his arrival in the Caribbean, Spanish privateers seized one of his ships, the ketch *Saint Francois*. Not only hostility from the external enemy, Spain, but also internal dissension and defections plagued La Salle's expedition. At long last, on February 20, 1685, he landed the colonists at Matagorda Bay. His misfortune was not to end there, however, for in the process of seeking a landing his storeship, the *Aimable*, became grounded at the mouth of the bay. Disheartened, its crew and several colonists returned to France with the naval vessel *Joly*. This left only one ship of the original four, the bark *Belle*. About a year later, in the winter of 1686, this ship also would meet a deleterious fate. Succumbing to the awesome force of a Texas squall, the *Belle* washed ashore, grounded and irretrievably broken.

In addition to the troubles already mentioned, the major problem left for La Salle to solve was fundamental: Where was he? Soon realizing that he had missed the Mississippi, he ordered the establishment of a structure that he named Fort St. Louis, off either Garcitas Creek in present Victoria County or off the Lavaca River in Jackson County. The next order of business consisted of a mini expedition to search by land for the great river. Interestingly, La Salle's first journey carried him west, to the Rio Grande. His initial thrust in a westerly direction raises intriguing questions, the answers to which are still in dispute among scholars of the subject.

One theory is that La Salle was searching for the silver mines of New Spain. It is true that the French were aware that the Spaniards had, by that time, opened a lucrative trade in silver in the upper reaches of New Spain. Therefore, so the story goes, La Salle was on a not-so-secret mission to establish a French presence in the area of France's perennial enemy, Spain, as a springboard to eventual occupation of those mines.

Another possibility as to why La Salle landed where he did is, in its own way, intriguing. It seems that in 1683, as he was exploring the mouth of the Mississippi, he concluded that the maps of his day charting the general region were wrong. He failed, apparently, to give serious consideration to the fact that his compass was broken and his astrolabe was giving erroneous latitudes. Left to his own devices, he took the sun as his focus, albeit with the limiting factor of intermittent cloudiness. Following his own devices, he concluded that the Mississippi was far to the west of the consensus of the day. The good news was that La Salle did not, at first, consider himself lost. The bad news was that he was indeed lost.

There remains yet a third possibility as to why La Salle failed to land on the banks of the Mississippi. This view rests not with any serious miscalculations about the proper route across the Gulf. Rather, the problem lay in La Salle's initial assumption that the Gulf surface currents had carried his ships far to the east of the Mississippi. In his much-celebrated book published in 1998, entitled *The La Salle Expedition to Texas*, researcher William Foster explains: "Unknown to the French at that time, the Gulf surface currents move westward, not eastward, during the winter months in the area the small French fleet crossed and in the coastal area La Salle first reached."

At any rate, La Salle's unproductive trip to the Rio Grande left him convinced that he had miscalculated. Therefore, upon returning to his base near Matagorda Bay to regroup, he engaged in two or three extended trips to the east, the farthermost reaching all the way to Louisiana but not quite to the Mississippi. On the last trip, a conspiratorial cadre of his expedition lured him into a trap and assassinated him on March 19, 1687.

In his classic article on the subject in the *Southwestern Historical Quarterly*, the legendary historian Herbert Bolton stated thusly: "Historians have supposed that this act [the murder of La Salle] was committed near the Trinity or the Neches, but evidence now available makes it quite clear that the spot was between the Brazos and Navasota rivers, and near the present city of Navasota."

In *The La Salle Expedition to Texas*, William Foster states the following: "This study concludes that Bolton's original designation…was basically accurate: La Salle was killed near the junction of the Brazos…and the Navasota Rivers."

Bolton and Foster based their analyses on studies of the diary of a member of La Salle's expedition, Henri Joutel. The key lies in a correct interpretation of which river Joutel labeled as the Canoe. Those endorsing the Navasota area as the site of La Salle's death interpret the Canoe as a reference to the Brazos, while those arguing for somewhere at or near the Trinity maintain that the Canoe refers to the Trinity.

Departing from Fort St. Louis on his fateful last journey, La Salle had left some twenty colonists behind. These consisted, for the most part, of women and children, the physically handicapped and those generally out of favor with La Salle. Taking advantage of the situation, upon learning of La Salle's death, the local Indians attacked the fort around Christmas 1688—according to Robert Weddle, "sparing only the children."

The Indians who attacked Fort St. Louis were the Karankawa, a tribe ranging roughly from the Lavaca River to Galveston Island. Known as cannibals, for religious purposes, the Karankawa would tie their victims to a stake with a fire burning thereby and ritualistically, bit by bit, tear the flesh from their bones and consume it, even as the victim watched in horror and pain.

The Spanish learned of La Salle's intrusion into the land of the Karankawa from captured pirates who, it turned out, were deserters from La Salle's expedition. Greatly alarmed, the Spanish authorized five sea voyages and six land marches seeking to locate the French intruders. Finally, on April 22, 1689, their persistence paid off. Success beckoned to the Spanish. An expedition under the leadership of Alonso de León came upon the ruins of Fort St. Louis. Of pivotal importance to the history of Texas, during this visit, a happenstance meeting with the Caddo Indians linked to the Blue Nun motivated the Spanish to establish a mission to the east.

In 1690, this same Alonso de León headed an expedition including, notably, Father Damián Massanet, who had accompanied de León to the fort the year before. Some twenty miles northeast of present Crockett, they established Mission San Francisco de las Tejas. The word *tejas* reflects the word *tayshas* of the Hasinai branch of the Caddo, among whom the Spanish established the mission. *Tayshas* was the Hasinai greeting that meant, essentially, "Welcome, friends." It is from *tayshas*, which in Spanish is *tejas*, that we get the anglicized word Texas.

THE BLUE NUN: THE PULL

A common element in the Spanish and Hasinai past was the legend of the Blue Nun. Let's hear what the executive secretary and editor of the Texas Folklore Society had to say about the first meeting between Father Massanet and the Tejas at La Salle's abandoned fort, the year before the Spanish established the mission:

> *Massanet had come to New Spain and Texas following tales of the miracles of Mother Maria de Agreda, Spain. Mother Maria had, through the miracle of bilocation, visited the land of the Tejas, or Caddos, without leaving her convent in Spain.*
>
> [At La Salle's fort, in 1689] *the Tejas told Father Damian that they were familiar with the stories of God, his Son, and the Holy Mother. They*

asked that he send missionaries among them to teach them Christianity as a "lady in blue" had taught them years before when she had come to their villages. Father Damian returned the following year [and] *founded Mission San Francisco de las Tejas.*

Furthermore, once at the mission, a Hasinai leader approached Father Damián asking for blue cloth for a burial shawl for his mother. Surprised, Damián asked the reason for the request. The Indian replied that his mother had spoken favorably of her encounter with the lady in blue years before.

Estimates are that some sixty thousand Texas Indians found Christianity due to the story of the Blue Nun. For our story, the Blue Nun and La Salle were complementary forces, pushing and pulling the Spanish to a site where the name of Texas took root, twin pillars conditioning the appellation of the Cradle of Texas Road.

CHAPTER 4

INDIGENOUS PEOPLES

ere we will begin with a survey of prehistoric Montgomery County and proceed through the rise of the Republic of Texas.

Prehistoric Times

What we know about the ingenuity and courage of the earliest people of our area boggles the mind. On a daily basis, the challenges consuming them would dwarf most of ours in a lifetime. Let's take a glimpse into the life and times of our forbearers in prehistoric Montgomery County.

Samplings have been found in original Montgomery County linked to cultures ranging from the Paleo-Americans of the late Pleistocene, or ice age, through cultures with characteristics of the Archaic era. These cultures collectively cover a prehistoric time span from about 12,000 BC to 2500 BC.

Especially mind-boggling were the Paleo-Americans, who, with the crudest of weapons, brought down such large and dangerous animals as mammoths, a type of early elephant, and saber-toothed tigers. The culture of these intelligent and robust people evolved from the earlier Clovis era to the Folsom, terms derived from the New Mexico towns where evidence of them first surfaced.

Thousands of years before the invention of bows and arrows, both Clovis and Folsom cultures featured the spear as the tool for hunting. Hunters of each culture attached their respective variety of sharpened stone as a dart to a foreshaft, which, in turn, was attached to a longer wooden shaft. When they thrust a spear into prey, the foreshaft and stone point would break off, remaining lodged in the animal.

By the Archaic era, the larger animals had perished, either from the dramatic change in climate, disease or over-hunting. Archaic peoples were also somewhat more settled than their Paleo-American forebears.

The weapon in common use during the Archaic period was the *atlatls*, a thin leather device of some twenty inches with which to propel a spear into a target. The hunter would first hook the *atlatls* to the wooden spear at the end opposite the spear's stone dart. Then, with one hand, he would both secure the remaining end of the *atlatls* and grasp the spear. Thus positioned, the hunter could fling the spear into a target with greater force than with just his bare hands.

Samplings of the Archaic culture were found in deep sand along Atkins Creek, just west of Conroe. Feverishly, scientists worked the scene. But alas, on the verge of surely major finds, the waters of the new Lake Conroe overtook them.

The culture of our immediate region was slow to emerge completely from the Archaic era. Until around AD 500, it was in what some call an "ethnological sink," stuck between the rising Caddo civilization to the east and a more primitive region called the "Galveston Bay Focus."

It is stirring to the mind to attune to the echoes of original Montgomery County's prehistoric past. Now let's survey the Native Americans in our area immediately before and during the era of the original Montgomery County.

To the northeast, near the Trinity, were branches of the Caddo, a tribe native to the area farther east, across the river. To the northwest roamed the Tonkawa and, of course, the ever-present Comanche on many occasions. To the southwest, occasionally making an appearance were the cannibalistic Karankawa. One would do well never to get on the wrong side of this tribe. Upon tying a victim to a post before a fire, designated women received the charge to eat the victim's flesh, a little at a time, even as the victim watched his life being dribbled away from him.

To the southeast, in the area of the present Woodlands, were the Orquoquisac. Let's look at an exotic tale of a Frenchman who suffered captivity at the hands of that tribe. In the summer of 1719, a French ship lost its way in the Caribbean, running aground near Galveston Island. While five men were ashore reconnoitering the site, the ship lost its mooring, leaving the men stranded. By the next year, all the seamen except one, named Simars de Bellisle, had succumbed to death. Herein lies an exotic Indian story of our area.

Bellisle managed to survive by eating such things as oysters, boiled grass and huge worms extracted from logs. As warm weather approached, members of the Orquoquisac tribe came upon him. These Indians habitually would go to the coast in the summer, to eat much the same thing Bellisle had been consuming; then in winter they would venture north. Their ramblings carried them to camps along Spring Creek and tributaries reaching to the southeastern fringes of later Grimes County.

The Orquoquisac made Bellisle a slave to a widow of the tribe, subjecting him to continual beatings. He was fortunate to be left alive. One can only imagine the first time he experienced one of the Orquoquisac "wailing greetings." Bellisle later wrote: "When morning came, they made me embark with them and they took me to the shore....When I arrived there, I heard these people...yell frightfully. This made me tremble and I thought they would kill me at any moment." He went on to say that "their custom was to yell as well for good as for bad news."

Eventually Bellisle had the good fortune of meeting a group of the Bidai (pronounced "bee dye") Indians, a more amenable tribe native to later Montgomery County. The Frenchman gave the Bidai a note requesting that they give it "to the first white men" they happened across. The Bidai were able, finally, to deliver the fortunate Frenchman to members of his own kind.

Germane to our study is a dramatic episode in the mid-eighteenth century, which engaged both the Orquoquisac and the Bidai within territory of the original Montgomery County, with overtones stretching to the present.

In the mid-eighteenth century, the area stretching from the lower Trinity River to the San Jacinto and along Spring Creek near the present Woodlands marked the center of a geopolitical battle between Spain and France. Occupying this region were the two prominent tribes of the area that would become Montgomery County, the Bidai and the Orquoquisac. These tribes played pivotal roles in the Spanish plans.

By the eve of the 1750s, the boundary between French Territory and the Spanish was in hot dispute. From their base in Louisiana, the French were trading with Indians to beyond the Trinity River, claiming rights from the explorations of the shipwrecked René-Robert Cavelier, Sieur de La Salle, in the mid-1680s. To the Spanish, this was outrageous.

Taking action, the Spanish leader of the fortress at La Bahia off Matagorda Bay, Joaquín Orobio Basterra, launched an expedition to the distant Spanish outposts in the east. On his return, approaching the vicinity of the Trinity, he stopped at a Bidai village called Santa Rosa de Viterbo. There he learned of a French presence off a river between the Trinity and the Brazos but tributary of neither.

Following Bidai directions, Captain Orobio crossed the Trinity to arrive on March 15, 1746, at a dwelling of Orquoquisac Indians, which he called San Rafael. Here he commissioned a guide who led him to the river in question, which he named Nuestra Señora de Aranzazu. After a brief reconnaissance of the area, Orobio returned to La Bahia. During the regime of Governor Jacinto de Barrios y Jáuregui between 1751 and 1759, the Spanish traded clandestinely along that river.

Feeling yet more threatened by the French, Governor Barrios commissioned a surveyor named Bernardo de Miranda to explore the area along a stream that merged with the Aranzazu, intent upon establishing a Spanish presence in the area. Miranda named the stream along which he explored Santa Rosa del Alcazar.

Upon obtaining Miranda's recommendations, the governor proposed to establish along the stream a community complex comprising Spanish and Tlascaltecan Indians. Plans included an order to transplant the Orquoquisac tribes of Chiefs Calzones Colorado and Canos to the new location on the Santa Rosa. The same order included measures to shield the Orquoquisac chieftain Mateo and his people from French machinations of trade and intrigue.

However, the brightness began to fade as pernicious quarreling and bureaucratic inertia ensued. By 1757, Barrios began to disfavor the project he had earlier sanctioned. Eventually, the plan met failure. However, the enterprise held repercussions for the present, as the river Nuestra Señora de Aranzazu took the name of San Jacinto, probably for Governor Jacinto de Barrios, although some say its namesake was the hyacinth plant. Meanwhile, Santa Rosa de Alcazar became known as Spring Creek.

By the time the Anglo-Americans came into this region, the Bidai were generally considered to be a rather docile tribe, friendly to the newcomers, for the most part. There was, for example, the case of a pioneer family's good fortune that when the father was away on business, a Bidai brave would protect his family—as was the case with Jesse Grimes, for whom Grimes County would receive its name.

Typical of stories of the Bidai at the time of the Anglo-American occupation of the area was a scenario played out at the home of Jacob Shannon, an early pioneer. Some Bidai were said to come to the Shannon homestead in the evenings during milking time with bowls. Upon drinking milk poured in the bowls, courtesy of the Shannons, the Indians would leave the bowls as payment.

Caddo Mound
State Park near
Nacogdoches.
*Courtesy of Caddo
Mound State Park.*

In reality, however, in earlier days the Bidai were known as the sovereign tribe of the whole state of Texas. Our information comes from a diary of a Mexican general named Manuel de Mier y Teran who headed an official expedition to Texas in 1828. The general recorded that the chief of the Bidai claimed that his tribe owned all of Texas, "including all the land, the waters, and the buffalo, deer, and turkeys." Furthermore, the general stated, "What does seem certain is that the Bidai really should be considered the original or among the oldest savages in Texas."

Yet another amazing fact surfaced with a review of the diary of General Mier y Teran. The Bidai were the true architects of the great Caddo Mounds of East Texas.

The true significance of these claims of the Bidai is brought into focus with the research of one Guy E. Powell. In 1967, this former naval commander wrote a compelling book entitled *Latest Aztec Discoveries*, isolating evidence that Aztlan, the original home of the Aztecs, lay just east of the original Montgomery County. A branch tribe of these forbearers of the Aztecs lived across a great river to the west. That would place the area in the land of the Bidai. Should Powell's thesis be correct, this would fuel educated speculation that the Bidai was that tribe.

Far from being just a docile folk who begged for milk, our Bidai once claimed sovereignty over the whole area later known as the great state of Texas, and possibly more.

Another tribe very key to the history of the original Montgomery County area is the Alabama-Coushatta. By 1780 they were knocking on the door of Texas, after first siding with the French in the old south. Once into Texas, they settled largely in East Texas but made a mark on the Trans-Brazos-Trinity basin through several prominent trails, called Coushatta traces. It

Coushatta
performing.
*Courtesy
of Joy
Montgomery.*

was along these that much of the Anglo-American Settlement followed. Along these trails were occasional Coushatta villages.

More will be said about these Native Americans in the next chapter, as they played key roles in the first three efforts to establish a free Texas Republic, and they continue until today as major players in Texas.

CHAPTER 5

FIRST AND SECOND TEXAS REPUBLICS, 1813 AND 1819

I n 1812, the first declaration of an independent Republic of Texas was made near present Madisonville. Our journey begins at the intersection of Highway 90 and the Old San Antonio Road (OSR), now Highway 21. Along the OSR from Madisonville east to the Trinity River were staged dramatic events surrounding both the birth and final demise of the First Republic of Texas. A marker east of Midway, between Madisonville and the Trinity, tells the story succinctly. We will relay the words of the marker and then expand upon the story the marker summarizes.

SITE OF TRINIDAD

Later known as Spanish Bluff, a fort and town as early as 1805. Captured by the Magee-Gutiérrez Expedition in October 1812. Near here the survivors of the Battle of Medina were executed in 1813. Inhabitants of the town were butchered by order of the Spanish commander and the town desolated.

The full name of Trinidad was Santissima Trinidad de Salcedo. The Magee-Gutiérrez Expedition cited on the marker referenced a group of Anglo-Americans, Native Americans and Tejanos termed the "Republican Army of the North." While in Trinidad in October 1812, they first declared Texas a state free of Spanish control—from the Trinity to the Sabine River.

SITE OF
TRINIDAD

LATER KNOWN AS SPANISH BLUFF • A
FORT AND TOWN AS EARLY AS 1805 •
CAPTURED BY THE MAGEE-GUTIERREZ
EXPEDITION IN OCTOBER, 1812 • NEAR
HERE THE SURVIVORS OF THE BATTLE
OF THE MEDINA WERE EXECUTED IN
1813 • INHABITANTS OF THE TOWN WERE
BUTCHERED BY ORDER OF THE SPANISH
COMMANDER AND THE TOWN DESOLATED

Erected by the State of Texas
1936

Trinidad marker off Highway 21.
Courtesy of Robin Montgomery.

By April 1813, the group had conquered San Antonio, the Spanish capital of Texas. Declaring the whole state free on April 6, they then proceeded to draw up the constitution on the seventeenth of that month. Truly a multicultural marvel, this, the First Republic of Texas, featured a Green Irish flag flying over a Tejano-Anglo state.

The foundation of the Green Flag Republic lay in the drive of the "Father of Mexico," Miguel Hidalgo, to free all of Mexico from the Spanish. As a lowly parish priest, on September 16, 1810, Hidalgo had called his mostly Indian followers to form an army and march toward Mexico City. Once there, alarmed by the destruction he saw, Hidalgo turned his army north, where, as a lieutenant colonel in Hidalgo's army, the later president of the Green Flag Republic, Don Bernardo Gutiérrez de Lara, began his quest for freedom. Acting on direct orders from Hidalgo himself, Gutiérrez traveled to the United States to secure aid. Upon an audience with the U.S. secretary of state, James Monroe, he recruited a force with U.S. army officer Augustus Magee, the originator of the green flag, in command.

Significant to these events was the wife of Don Bernardo, Doña María Josefa Uribe Gutiérrez. Staying behind with her family throughout the ordeal of the rise and fall of the First Republic of Texas, she exhibited great courage even in suffering removal from her home at the hands of Spanish authorities. Truly, Doña María was a magnificent original first lady of Texas, although her time in the position was short.

Significant to the story of the Green Flag Republic was its multicultural makeup. Even with a strong Mexican Catholic heritage behind him, Don Bernardo yet recruited an army of citizens from the United States, a nation with Anglo-Protestant roots. Not only were those roots Protestant, but they were riding the crest of the Second Great Awakening.

Exhibiting a grand degree of togetherness, the group also received substantial support from the Alabama-Coushatta Indians from in and around later original Montgomery County territory. That combination brought in some three hundred warriors to fight for the cause of Texas independence in 1812 and 1813. Additionally, there was at least one African American from the United States.

As Don Bernardo approached San Antonio, seeking local support via pamphlets, he emphasized the multicultural mix of his army, as expressed below:

> *Rise en masse, soldiers and citizens: unite in the holy cause of our country! I am now marching to your succor with a respectable force of American volunteers who left their homes and families to take up our cause, to fight for our liberty. They are the free descendants of the men who fought for the independence of the United States: and as brothers and inhabitants of the same continent they have drawn their swords with a hearty good will in the defense of the cause of humanity: and in order to drive the tyrannous Europeans beyond the Atlantic.*

Unfortunately, on August 4, 1813, internal politics forced Don Bernardo to yield the leadership of the Green Flag Republic to José Álvarez de Toledo. Only when this change in their government brought a realignment of their politics, resulting in its army isolating the units according to race, did the Army of the First Republic lose a major battle.

Awesome was that loss, however, at the Battle of Medina on August 18, 1813, marking the worst defeat ever recorded on Texas soil. As indicated on the marker at the beginning of this chapter, after the battle, Spanish troops pursued the remnants of the Texas army to Trinidad, near present Madisonville, and proceeded to demolish both the remains of the Green Flag Army and the town and citizens of Trinidad.

The great lesson of the First Republic of Texas is "united we stand, divided we fall."

The James Long Expedition, 1819

While Don Bernardo Gutiérrez had suffered release from his position of president of the First Republic of Texas before the Battle of Medina, he continued to engage the winds of revolution in Texas. As a result, he was slated to take the position of vice president in a second effort to create a free Texas Republic, under the directorship of Dr. James Long. The motivation for this effort lay in the agreement between the United States and Spain to make the Sabine River the eastern boundary of Spanish Texas.

Many persons in the United States contended that the United States did not have the power to bargain away the greater part of East Texas to the Spanish. Their claim lay, ultimately, in the Louisiana Purchase from France in 1803, due to which—based on the La Salle expedition, addressed in Chapter 2—France, and thereby the United States, held a claim to the Rio Grande as the Texas border due to the La Salle expedition's initial trip to that river. A contingent of the group, led by Dr. James Long, initiated a filibustering expedition into Texas before official word of the boundary agreement leaked out.

Dr. Long convened seventy-five followers at Natchez, Mississippi, in the summer of 1819 to make their way to Nacogdoches. By the time they reached Nacogdoches, he had accumulated a force of over three hundred men. His objective, as with the previous "Republican Army of the North," lay in possessing the country, forming a government and inviting settlers to join him.

Accordingly, Long's first step upon occupying the country consisted of establishing a supreme council of eleven members. Among these was Gutiérrez de Lara, who, as already mentioned, was cast as the vice president of the proposed new republic. Among other items, Long sent Major Cook to a settlement on the Red River called Pecan Point.

At the time, Pecan Point was already the abode of at least Andrew Montgomery and J.G.W. Pierson, forerunners of many settlers who would soon make the area of Pecan Point their staging ground for later original Montgomery County. These included the Montgomery family of William and his sons Edley and John, brothers of Andrew, along with daughters Anne, Mary Jane, Sara and Elizabeth; Elizabeth would become the wife of J.G.W. Pierson. Also among these settlers were the Greenwoods, Henry Bailey and his sons, Franklin and Joel, who married daughters of William Montgomery, Anne and Mary Jane. Other Montgomery Countians included Peter Cartwright, later of Bear Bend near Montgomery.

The next task for the Long expedition lay in fortifying the area. It was to this end that the territory of the later original Montgomery County came into play, for the filibusters established four forts, two each along the later eastern border of the county, the Trinity River, and the western boundary, the Brazos. In charge of the upper Trinity was David Long, brother of Dr. James Long, while the lower section of that river constituted the camp of Major Smith among the Coushatta Indians at the end of one of the Coushatta traces in the later county. Near the Falls of the Upper Brazos went Captain Johnson, while Captain Walker was placed near the later town of Washington-on-the-Brazos at the end of the Coushatta trace.

In order to enhance the security of his government, Dr. Long set out for Galveston Island to confer with the pirate Jean Lafitte. En route to this conference, while passing through the Coushatta village, he received word of an approaching Spanish force under the command of Colonel Ignacio Pérez. Long immediately dispatched orders to his outposts to congregate at the Coushatta village, while he hastened on his journey to Galveston.

Meanwhile, the Spanish attacked the post of Captain Johnson, taking eleven prisoners while the rest of them fled down the river to Walker's position. Soon this group also suffered an attack by the more than three hundred Spanish soldiers. The Republicans fled through the territory of later Montgomery County by way of the lower Coushatta trace to the village of Indians for whom the trace had been named. The Spaniards pursued them in an indirect manner, going first to the camp of David Long, then to Nacogdoches. After successes at these two sites, Pérez routed the remnants of the Long expedition by now congregated at Smith's camp. After this, surviving Republicans gathered at Point Bolivar, near Galveston.

By the next year, Long had gathered another army, which eventually also met defeat, but this one had little to do with later Montgomery County.

CHAPTER 6

THREE STAGES OF
THE TEXAS REVOLUTION

I n this chapter we will explore the various stages leading to the great Battle of San Jacinto, along with noting representative residents of the area of original Montgomery County who participated in these events.

STAGE ONE OF THE TEXAS REVOLUTION

The restlessness of the Texans east of the Brazos reached revolutionary proportions in response to the Law of April 6, 1830. Among other things, the law prohibited further colonization of Texas by Americans and provided for the garrisoning of Mexican troops in the state to enforce customs and collections.

The first revolutionary scene resulted from the actions of the custom collector for the ports east of the Colorado, George Fisher, who set up his customhouse at Anahuac at the head of Galveston Bay. This was near where Mexico's John Bradburn held command of the military post. Fisher issued a decree requiring shipmasters leaving Texas from nearby ports to secure clearances from him at Anahuac before sailing. In some cases, this required Texans to make a two-hundred-mile trip overland before sailing. Mexicans canceled this procedure after a mini skirmish near the mouth of the Brazos.

A more serious threat occurred in 1831 when Francisco Madero came to Texas from Mexico clothed with authority to grant land titles to settlers east of the San Jacinto. Bradburn ordered Madero to desist on the ground that he was violating the Law of 1830 and proceeded to arrest him.

Insecurity converged into action as the Texans threatened to attack Bradburn. Key instigators of this action were William B. Travis and Patrick Jack. The latter was a landowner and citizen of later Anderson, in original Montgomery County territory. Upon Bradburn's arrest of these individuals, John Austin convened around 160 men at Liberty. Among those gathered was J.H. Shepperd of Montgomery, who at this time began what proved to be a most eventful four-year revolutionary experience. The actual skirmish was slight. However, from it developed two important consequences: the departure of Bradburn for Mexico and the Battle of Velasco.

After John Austin and his small army left Anahuac, they stopped at Brazoria long enough to load three cannons on a boat before returning to Anahuac. En route, they met a Mexican force in Velasco. The ensuing Battle of Velasco resulted in the riddance of Mexican troops from the Anglo-American part of Texas. One of the members of Austin's force was Allen Larrison of High Point near present Stoneham, in original Montgomery County territory. Larrison was a schoolteacher who would later fight at the Battle of San Jacinto. Another was Charles Stewart; more on Stewart later.

Even as these events unfolded, in Mexico Santa Anna was seeking the overthrow of President Anastasio Bustamante. Apprehensive of the Texan's attitude, Santa Anna sent General Mexia to investigate. On the latter's trip, Stephen F. Austin accompanied him, addressing to him the "Turtle Bayou Resolutions," a declaration of June 13, 1832, expressing Texan support for Santa Anna.

Also, during this first stage of the revolution, two conventions occurred in as many years in an attempt to further stabilize the situation. The first of these is known as the convention of the Texas "Peace Party" and was headed by Stephen F. Austin. The group compiled a list of grievances against the Mexican government. High on this list were the desire for land titles, the repeal of the prohibition of Anglo-American immigration and the admission of Texas to the Mexican Confederation as a separate state from Coahuila. To the chagrin of the Texans, the Mexican government refused to accept this list of grievances.

This refusal rekindled the emotions of the radical element in the Texas camp. Consequently, in 1833, the second convention assembled. This time the chairmanship went to the leader of the "War Party" faction, William H. Wharton. Under Wharton's leadership, the gathering composed essentially the same petition as the Convention of 1832, while it added a model constitution for Texas based on that of the United States. It is important to the history of Texas and Montgomery County that Sam Houston chaired the committee to draw up the constitution. Among those attending the convention with Houston who had interests in the area of later Montgomery County were William Robinson, Jared Groce, Joshua Hadley, Francis Holland and Jesse Grimes.

Though the Mexican government again failed to act positively on the Texans' petitions, Texans remained relatively quiet for approximately the next eighteen months, thereby ending the first stage of the revolution. There were several external and internal reasons for this. In the former category were several reforms that the Mexican government initiated: it was during this interval that it completed the division of Texas into three departments with capitals, at Bexar (or San Antonio), Nacogdoches and San Felipe, respectively. Also, Texas received three deputies of the twelve that composed the state congress. Furthermore, the English language became recognized for official purposes, and the court system received recognition. Further serving as a respite from political intrigue was an epidemic of cholera and malaria, along with severe floods.

STAGE TWO OF THE TEXAS REVOLUTION

In October 1835, this tranquility abruptly changed as Mexico discarded federalism and officially established a centralist regime. The situation in Texas, which coincided with this event, became inflammatory. The capital of the state government of Coahuila and Texas had been established in Saltillo. However, the city of Monclova challenged Saltillo for that honor. When Santa Anna sided with Monclova, Saltillo attempted to move its facilities to Bexar. At this show of impudence, Santa Anna sent his brother-in-law, Martin Perfecto de Cos, to enforce Monclova's claims. Along the way, the claims of Saltillo received a new look.

As these events unfolded, on October 2 and following, Texans at Gonzales repelled two thrusts from San Antonio aimed at retrieving a cannon decorated with the fighting words "Come and Take It." On October 9, the Mexican garrison at Goliad fell to a Texan force, led by George Collinsworth, blocking the route from San Antonio to the coast. On October 12, Stephen F. Austin arrived from imprisonment in Mexico to take military command at Gonzales, ordering the Texan forces "on to San Antonio."

On October 28, at the Battle of Mission Concepción, a ninety-man expeditionary force under James Fannin and James Bowie defeated four hundred Mexicans near Mission Concepción. In this battle were Joseph

L. Bennett, S.H. Shepperd and Matthew Cartwright, all from the later Montgomery County area. During this siege, Texans attacked a Mexican force believed to be carrying silver, which turned out to be grass for the horses. In this "grass fight" from later Montgomery County were W.S. Taylor, Richard Williams, John Major Williams, S.H. Shepperd and George Washington Robinson. A final assault at this time under "Ole Ben Milam" included Zoroaster Robinson from later Montgomery County and John S. Black from the area of later Anderson.

Permanent Council, October 11–30

Meanwhile, on the political scene, provisional governments were seeking to organize and support the armed forces. The first of these, known as the Permanent Council, convened from October 11 to 30, 1835. It consisted of the Committee of Safety of San Felipe and other communities. Among its accomplishments, it sent supplies and volunteers to the army, set up a postal system, ordered land offices closed, authorized an agent to the United States to borrow $100,000 and, in general, acted as a clearinghouse for information. The president of the Permanent Council was Richard Royall, while his secretary was Charles B. Stewart of Montgomery.

Headstone of the Reverend Daniel Parker. He performed probably the first formal wedding in the Cradle Road area, marrying Henry Fanthorp and Rachel Kennard. *Public domain.*

On October 17, the Permanent Council created a Committee of Five to establish the Texas Rangers, positioned to patrol the area including the original Montgomery County between the Brazos and the Trinity. Involved with this decision were Silas Parker and J.G.W. Pierson, while Daniel Parker chaired the committee.

CONSULTATION: NOVEMBER 1–14

On November 1, 1835, the Permanent Council yielded to the "Consultation of the Chosen Delegates of All of Texas, in General Convention Assembled." The fundamental question of the delegates from the twelve municipalities of the Departments of the Brazos and Department of Nacogdoches was: For what were they fighting? The answer lay in the Mexican Constitution of 1824, which had established a federal system of government.

Additionally, the Consultation endorsed the work of the Permanent Council, adopted a plan for the creation of an army and elected Sam Houston commander-in-chief of the regular army. Then they drew up a plan for the organization of a provisional government. Signing the "Texas Declaration of Causes for taking up arms against Mexico" and the document establishing a provisional government was J.G.W. Pierson.

Also at the Consultation from the original Montgomery County area were Jesse Grimes, later to become the first chief justice of Montgomery County and namesake of Grimes County, along with Dr. B.B. Goodrich of Anderson and Elijah Collard.

PROVISIONAL GOVERNMENT: NOVEMBER 15, 1835–MARCH 1, 1836

Here the governor was Henry Smith, with James W. Robinson as lieutenant governor. The venerable Charles B. Stewart was again secretary. Notably, during Stewart's tenure, the governor and lieutenant governor were in conflict, with Henry Smith actually being impeached. Smith's view of Stewart during this period is an indication of the high moral character of Charles Stewart:

> *Mr. Stewart was very conscientious and scrupulously honest on all his dealings, both of a private and public nature. When the General Council*

Charles Stewart, Texas's first secretary of state and more, is featured here at the Conroe Flag Park; Craig Campobella, sculptor. *Courtesy of YourConroeNews.com.*

demanded that the records of his office be turned over to them, he refused without displaying anger or concern. When they attempted to discharge him for refusing to obey their demands, he continued to perform his duties as if nothing had occurred, merely informing me of these happenings without comment.

Joining Stewart in the provisional government from the original Montgomery County area were Jesse Grimes and J.G.W. Pierson.

CONVENTION, WASHINGTON-ON-THE-BRAZOS: MARCH 1–17

The delegates met at Washington-on-the-Brazos, with making official their drive for independence on their minds. On the evening of the first day, a group under the leadership of George Childress of Tennessee adjourned across the Brazos to Groce's Retreat, in later original Montgomery County territory. There they edited the sample Texas Declaration of Independence brought by Childress, to be voted on the next day. Hence, on March 2, 1836, Texas officially declared its independence.

A few days later, Sam Houston received the title of major general in charge of all military forces. This was a step up for him, as earlier, at the Consultation, he had been made commander of the regular, but not volunteer, forces.

As the convention began, there were twenty-three municipalities in Texas, political entities similar to counties in the Mexican system. On March 17, the delegates declared these municipalities to be counties. One of those counties was Washington County, successor to Washington Municipality.

Here is a major story of Montgomery County, for the leader, or alcalde, of Washington Municipality was Joshua Hadley, whose home was near Roans Prairie in original Montgomery County territory. A regidor, or councilman, in Hadley's government was Jesse Grimes, while Abraham Zuber from near later Shiro was in the running. Jacob Shannon of Montgomery and A.D. Kennard from near Roans Prairie were in the running for sheriff of the municipality.

STAGE THREE: THE ALAMO AND SAN JACINTO

Even as the delegates worked at Washington-on-the-Brazos, the Alamo fell on March 6. Involved in that tragic event from original Montgomery County were the son of Jesse Grimes, Charles Grimes, and the brother of Dr. B.B. Goodrich of Anderson, John G. Goodrich. Also to fall was Tapley Holland.

A major story from the lore of the Alamo was that of William B. Travis drawing a line in the sand on March 3, announcing that the end was inevitable, but all who chose to stay and fight to the death should cross the line. Tapley Holland was the first to answer the call. On that fateful day, only one man failed to cross the line, and he told his story at the home of Abraham Zuber, near present Shiro. His name was Moses Rose, a brave Frenchman who had already served in three previous engagements for Texas.

Among the survivors of the battle were Mrs. Susanna Dickinson and her infant daughter, Angelina. Angelina became known as the "Babe of the Alamo." Angelina Dickinson would later marry John Meynard Griffith and live awhile on the Griffith homestead just south of Dobbin.

Following the fall of the Alamo on March 6, 1836, came the Battle of San Jacinto on April 21, 1836. The primary standout of that battle, of course, was its commander, Sam Houston, a citizen of Huntsville. Other representatives of the area of the original county included Joseph L. Bennett, a lieutenant colonel, and captains of two companies, James Gillespie of Huntsville, Sixth Company, and William Ware of the Danville area, Second Company. Included in Gillespie's company were his in-laws, the brothers Andrew and

Hezekiah Farris cabin when off the courthouse square in Huntsville. It now stands in the Sam Houston Park across the road from Sam Houston State University. *Courtesy of Robin Montgomery.*

John Montgomery, and Gillespie's father-in law, Hezekiah Farris, along with Alphonso Steele.

In Ware's company were John Sadler, George W. Washington, Albert Gallatin, Matthew and William Cartwright and the brothers William, James W. and John F. Winters.

Of note is that both the first and the last Texans to die at San Jacinto—George Lamb and Alphonso Steele, respectively—were of original Montgomery County. Other representatives of the area included Allen Larrison and W.S. Taylor, while John M. Wade played a key role in managing the famous "twin sisters" cannons.

Significant to the battle were the baggage men, William Zuber, William McIntyre and William E. Kennard. J.H. Shepperd was part of the army but, directed to bargain with the Indians, he missed the battle itself. Finally, J.S. Black of Anderson did significant duty in managing the supply wagons for the army.

CHAPTER 7

A FEW DRAMATIC SAGAS OF THE LATTER REVOLUTIONARY ERA

I n the immediate interval between victory at San Jacinto and the birth of Montgomery County on December 14, 1837, several dramatic incidents took place in or with repercussions affecting our area. We will summarize three of those: (1) the Fort Parker massacre, (2) the tragedy of a mother and child due to Indian depredations in the original county and (3) more detail on the story of William B. Travis drawing the line in the sand at the Alamo. Additionally, we will address a composite of incidents related to the Noah Griffith family just below Dobbin.

THE FORT PARKER MASSACRE AND MONTGOMERY COUNTY

On May 19, 1836, several hundred Comanche and Kiowa Indian warriors attacked Fort Parker in present Limestone County, Texas. Herein was the framework upon which developed one of the most heartrending dramas in American history, a drama destined to delay until 1875 the closing of the Indian Wars in Texas. We will look at a few members of the remarkable Parker family and their connection linking Fort Parker to Montgomery County.

Daniel Parker was a preacher. With his brother, James W. Parker, he visited Mexican Texas in 1832, where he learned that he could not start a church in Texas. He could, however, return to the United States and start one, then

Both the beginning and results of Fort Parker are linked indelibly to our Cradle area. *Courtesy of Wikipedia.*

bring that church to Texas. This Daniel did, and he performed perhaps the first Christian wedding in Texas, marrying Henry Fanthorp and Rachel Kennard in what would later become known as Anderson.

Daniel was head of the committee at the Permanent Council in 1835 that created the Texas Rangers. His brother, Silas Parker, a ranger, first settled near present Stoneham. Later, Silas met his death at the Fort Parker massacre, while the Comanche took captive his son, John, and a daughter, Cynthia Ann. Cynthia Ann became the wife of the Comanche war chief and the mother of Quanah Parker, the last and greatest of the American Indian chiefs.

Also a ranger, as well as a preacher, was the brother of Silas and Daniel, James W. Parker. James W. brought his family to Grimes Prairie in the early 1830s before leaving to help establish Fort Parker. After the massacre, he escorted many survivors back to Montgomery County. In his later book, *The Rachel Plummer Narrative*, Parker formally thanked Jesse Grimes and Andrew Montgomery for helping these survivors restore their livelihood.

As an addendum to the story of the Parkers of Montgomery County, intrigue surrounds the journey of Lucy Parker, wife of Silas and mother of Cynthia Ann, and her son John. The story relates directly to the history of Montgomery County, centering on data in the Montgomery County Courthouse.

According to the Montgomery County *Probate Record Book*, the wife of Silas Parker, Lucy, administered Silas's will in Montgomery County, Texas, in 1836. According to the Montgomery County census, Lucy Parker in

1850 was living with a John Parker, whose birthdate was given as 1830. This birthdate coincides with that of the John Parker captured at the massacre, brother of Cynthia Ann and son of Lucy. Thus, the probability arises that John and his mother, Lucy Parker, spent their latter days in Montgomery County, probably watching with much interest the career of their grandson and nephew, respectively, the great Comanche chief Quanah Parker.

As administrators, legislators, Texas rangers, preachers and more, the Parkers of original Montgomery County were indeed a remarkable family.

THE SAGA OF MRS. TAYLOR

The Battle of San Jacinto, April 21, 1836, freed Texas from the dictatorial regime of Mexican president Santa Anna. Yet from that date until the birthdate of Montgomery County, December 14, 1837, constant vigilance remained a necessity for citizens of our area. One reason lay in Indian unrest, kindled largely by the continued machinations of Mexican forces. A glimpse of both the tragedy and the compassion of the era lies in the saga of Mrs. Taylor.

On March 8, 1837, two friends, Levi Taylor and Alex Whitaker, were cowhunting in the western portion of what would soon become Montgomery County. Suddenly, a band of Indians surprised them, taking the life of Levi, while Alex escaped to tell the tale. Accordingly, Levi's wife, whose first name has been lost to history, moved with her three children to the home of the former alcalde of Washington Municipality, Joshua Hadley. It was then that an even greater tragedy ensued.

On June 2, 1837, Indians attacked the Hadley home. Shortly thereafter, against the pleas of the Hadleys, Mrs. Taylor rushed with her three children toward the nearby home of the venerable Joseph L. Bennett, recently a lieutenant colonel at the Battle of San Jacinto. Seizing the opportunity, the Indians again attacked, killing not only Mrs. Taylor but also her little girl, while wounding one of her two sons. Nor did the tragic scene subside with these events, for in her dying moments, Mrs. Taylor gave birth to yet another child. The evidence available suggests that this child did not survive.

Though weary from continual war and strife, citizens of the area responded with compassion. Even while plans were being made to place the remaining Taylor children with their father's brother in Tennessee, others sought immediately to punish the perpetrators of the tragedy. A man named Kindred quickly rode his horse some thirty miles eastward to the village of Montgomery. Comparisons to the proverbial ride of Paul Revere are certainly in order, for Mr. Kindred arrived in Montgomery, secured the services of twenty-five intrepid souls and, with them, returned to Hadley's Prairie—the night of the same day he had left.

The next morning, the men embraced the great pursuit, traveling several hundred miles to the north. After a valiant effort, they surprised the Indians, who managed to escape, though they left behind most of their weapons, along with Mrs. Taylor's scalp.

A time of tragedy and compassion surrounded our county's birth.

THE "IMPOSTER" OF THE ALAMO

William B. Travis, intrepid warrior for Texas. *Courtesy of haikudeck.com.*

It was March 3, 1836. With overwhelming force, Mexican president and general Santa Anna surrounded the Alamo in San Antonio. Inside that mission complex, Colonels William B. Travis, David Crockett and James Bowie addressed their situation. It was hopeless, they agreed. Inevitable was their defeat. Accordingly, Travis assembled his men. Taking his sword, he drew a line in the sand. "Those who wish to stay, cross this line," he commanded.

Responding to Travis's challenge, all 190 fighting men in the Alamo crossed his line, led by Tapley Holland of our Cradle Road. Or did they? Was this whole scene just the figment of someone's imagination? The truth rests on several factors. Key to these is the veracity of William Zuber's account. On March 6, 1836, when the Alamo fell, with the consequent deaths of all the Texas combatants, William Zuber was with Sam Houston's army, preparing for what turned out to be the decisive battle for Texas's independence at San Jacinto. Thirty-seven years later, William Zuber would put the story of Travis drawing the line into print.

The next factor to consider is the source of Zuber's information, and this adds yet another twist to the story. For Zuber wrote that not every fighting man in the Alamo crossed the line on this fateful day. A Frenchman named Moses Rose refused to cross. Rather, Rose slipped away over the wall into the night, to eventually find rest and sustenance in the home of William Zuber's parents. Living near Shiro, Zuber's father, Abraham Zuber, later to become the first district clerk of Montgomery County, was an old friend of Moses Rose, having known him in Nacogdoches before the Texas Revolution.

Nestled in security with old friends, Rose revealed the story to which William Zuber fell heir on his return from San Jacinto. Rose related how, on the way to the Zubers', he had told the story one time and met with a bitter reaction, leading to his being labeled an imposter, the "Coward of the Alamo." Was it, therefore, in order to protect the reputation of his father's friend while he lived that Zuber waited until 1873 to put the story into print? Sources vary on Zuber's motives for writing.

But bear this in mind. Most sources agree that Moses Rose had fought bravely under Napoleon as the latter sought to become the ruler of Europe. Furthermore, Rose fought in three battles in Texas preliminary to the Alamo. Should Zuber's story of Rose leaving the Alamo ring true, it seems clear he did not leave because he was a coward.

Noah Griffith, Sandhill Cranes and the Babe of the Alamo

Shortly after his arrival from New York in 1830, just below the present town of Dobbin, Noah Griffith and his wife built a fine home, put together with wooden pegs and hewn inside with a dye to aid in sealing. Unfortunately, this house burned in 1898. Before that dreadful event, enacted in the area surrounding the Griffith home were multiple episodes of historic drama.

The first bit of drama came in the summer of 1832, at a time when Noah was away in Harrisburg securing supplies. He left his wife and young sons, ranging in age from two to eleven years old, at home. During Noah's absence, a band of Indians camped for several days near the house. Uneasy, Mrs. Griffith nailed the shutters closed, allowing the summer heat to stifle the refugees huddled inside. Compounding the heat-induced misery was hunger due to the lack of supplies.

While thus encumbered, great delight consumed the family at the sight, one day, of two sandhill cranes landing in the yard. Seizing the opportunity to save her family from starvation, Mrs. Griffith permitted Sercy, the eldest boy, to shoot one of the cranes; this provided the family's only nourishment until Noah returned. Though the nearby Indians never made any menacing moves, the story became a treasured heirloom of the family.

Later, in 1836, a dramatic event in faraway San Antonio sparked a cry around the world. This was "Remember the Alamo." The Alamo's "messengers of defeat" were Susanna Dickinson, widow of Captain Almaron Dickinson, and their infant daughter, Angelina, known to history as the "Babe of the Alamo." The invading Mexican general Santa Anna allowed Susanna to carry the message of the fall of the heroes, Travis, Crockett and company, to General Sam Houston, then camped at Gonzales.

Among the stories of the Babe's stay at the Alamo, it is said that William B. Travis tied his cat's-eye ring around the child's neck. Another—and an incredible—story concerned Angelina and the notorious Santa Anna himself. Initially, but for the intercession of Santa Anna's aide, Juan Almonte, the Babe and her mother would not have been spared. Santa Anna not only relented but also developed tender feelings for the child. Only the staunch refusal of her mother prevented Santa Anna from adopting Angelina!

The Babe of the Alamo led an eventful, if rather unhappy, life, as implied by several broken marriages. The first marriage, at age seventeen, at her mother's insistence, was to John Meynard Griffith, son of Noah Griffith. John Meynard and the Babe made their home for a few years just across from the Griffiths' historic homestead. Here she bore him three children, before leaving for adventure in New Orleans.

What stories the old Griffith home must have witnessed before its destruction by fire in 1898.

CHAPTER 8

ORIGINAL MONTGOMERY COUNTY

EVENTS AND PERSONALITIES

I t will be recalled that Montgomery County emerged from Washington County, which in turn had emerged from Washington Municipality. Accordingly, in this chapter we will survey this sequence, highlighting certain events and personalities along the way.

It was in July 1835 that Washington Municipality became a new municipality within the Department of the Brazos, which department had appeared in 1834 after the Departments of Nacogdoches in 1831 and San Antonio in 1824. Washington Municipality comprised an area of numerous later counties on both sides of the Brazos River. On the west were Washington, Brazos, Burleson and Lee Counties, while on the east was the total area of original Montgomery County, including all or parts of later Montgomery, Grimes, Walker, Madison, San Jacinto and Waller Counties.

The alcalde or director of Washington Municipality was, as mentioned in the last chapter, Joshua Hadley of Roans Prairie. The son of Benjamin and Elizabeth Hadley, Joshua Hadley came to Texas about 1830. Upon settling first in what became San Augustine County, he moved to a league of land just south of present Roans Prairie. Hadley also received a league to the north in Sterling Robertson's Colony. On his home property he built a two-story frame house and a log fort for the protection of his family and neighbors. During his stay at this home, Indians attacked, killing Mrs. Taylor, as mentioned in the previous chapter. Hadley was married to the former Obedience Grantham. They had five children, who joined the old Oakland Church of Roan's Prairie.

The members of the award-winning Jacob Austin band now reside on the site of the old Joshua Hadley homesite near the Hadley Fort. *Public domain.*

The Independence Convention in Washington created Washington County as part of the action turning all of Texas's twenty-three municipalities into counties. By February 13, 1837, Washington County was divided into six precincts, three on each side of the Brazos. On the west side were the precincts of Hazard, Hidalgo and Washington, while on the east were Viesca, Lake Creek and San Jacinto Precincts. Justices of the peace on the east were: for Viesca, A. McGuffin and J.L. Bennett; for Lake Creek, Jeremiah Worsham and George Galbraith; and for San Jacinto Precinct, William Roberts and William Robinson. John Montgomery was constable for Viesca.

Just after the Battle of San Jacinto, with residual trouble remaining from the immediate aftereffects of independence, Sam Houston appointed another citizen with an original Montgomery County connection to head a seventy-four-person militia. This was J.G.W. Pierson. Pierson could truthfully be described as an unsung hero of old Montgomery County.

J.G.W. Pierson

To the Texas senate in December 1836, Stephen F. Austin explained that the containment of hostile Indians to the north saved his southern colony, which included later Montgomery County, from "anarchy and civil war."

A major reason those tribes were contained was that J.G.W. Pierson was de facto leader of Sterling Robertson's Colony in that northern region. The area over which Pierson exercised authority was the scene of the fiercest Indian fighting in the history of Texas. Unmatched for valor and impact on our area's history, Pierson is also one of the fathers of Montgomery County.

The death of his second wife, Elizabeth Montgomery, in 1833, had prompted Pierson to go to Robertson's Colony, bent initially on directing the establishment of the city of Saraville de Viesca, at the time slated to become the capital of Texas. Pierson took with him a wealth of experience gained in Arkansas Territory before he came to Texas. He had served as sheriff, commander of militia and magistrate of the settlement of Pecan Point. His accomplishments included commanding the unit that removed the troublesome Shawnee from that territory—in a peaceful manner.

In 1835, Pierson represented the Municipality of Viesca at the Permanent Council Consultation in San Felipe de Austin. Here he served on the "Committee of Five," which gave birth to the Texas Rangers. In the same year, Pierson and a few friends founded the town of Independence, which became known as "the Athens of Texas," the original home of both Baylor and Mary Hardin Baylor Universities. Later Pierson founded a community he called High Point, near present Stoneham in original Montgomery County. As Mexican forces continued to threaten Texas, on June 30, 1836, Pierson received orders to provide security to settlers. It was on the following May 31, 1837, that Pierson became "Captain of Volunteers" of Washington County.

However, Pierson was not yet through helping Texas. In 1842, Mexican forces occupied San Antonio, prompting formation of the Alexander Somervell expedition of Texas militia. After securing the border with Mexico, Somervell ordered the army to disband. Pierson was among those who refused to leave, continuing under the command of Colonel William Fisher to pursue the Mexican army into Mexico. About this "Mier expedition," Fisher later wrote, "I found two of the smallest companies under the command of Captain Reese of Brazoria and Captain Pierson united to a man and prepared to fight to the last extremity. The others were in indescribable confusion."

Captured by the Mexicans, Pierson escaped, only to suffer captivity later. Fortunately, he drew a white bean at El Rancho Salado on March 25, 1843, an act that saved his life. Those unfortunate enough to draw a black bean met their death at the hands of Mexican troops.

Robin Montgomery playing the role of J.G.W. Pierson at the February 2021 Texas Independence Day celebration in Conroe. Montgomery depicted the multiple roles—political, military and social—of this amazing product of our history. The February celebration was sponsored by the Heritage Museum of Montgomery County when Joy Montgomery was its director. *Courtesy of the* Conroe Courier.

Along with Pierson during the Mexican crisis was his former brother-in-law and fellow officer earlier in Sterling Robertson's Colony, Andrew Montgomery, brother of Pierson's by-then-deceased wife, Elizabeth Montgomery. Andrew escaped the Black Bean affair as follows: before the capture of Pierson's company, he had volunteered to leave camp and search for food. In the process, he happened upon an African American man to whom he had earlier given bread from his scarce supplies. The man informed Andrew of the captivity of his colleagues and guided him to safety.

JESSE GRIMES

A neighbor to Andrew Montgomery and Pierson in the High Point area was Jesse Grimes of Grimes Prairie. After serving as a regidor, or councilman, in the government of Washington Municipality, Grimes started the process in the Texas legislature of making the area of original Montgomery County a legal political entity. Like Pierson, Grimes was a pivotal figure in the history of original Montgomery County. Grimes and his friend William B. Travis were major players in early Texas history who jointly set the stage for the birth of Montgomery County. Let's explore the basis for this declaration.

Jesse Grimes was born in North Carolina in 1788. By 1826, his first wife, Martha, had died, and he was married to the widow Rosanna Britton. Between his wives, he would sire fifteen children. It was in 1826 that the Jesse Grimes family settled briefly near San Felipe de Austin, the heart of Anglo-Texas government.

By 1827, Grimes had forged the path of Grimes Road from San Felipe to just beyond present Stoneham to make his new home, some thirty miles west of present Conroe. Continuing his ties to San Felipe, in the early 1830s, Jesse occupied several key positions in the District of Viesca, originally a vast governmental district associated with San Felipe and extending through the later original Montgomery County.

Along the way, Grimes made friends with a young man named William B. Travis, who developed a reputation as a firebrand in altercations with Mexican authorities at Anahuac. In 1834, Travis sent a letter to his friend Jesse Grimes, which read in part: "I have been charged to give notice to you of your appointment to the office of Judge of the first instance for the jurisdiction of Austin [Austin Municipality]."

In 1835 and 1836, Jesse Grimes played key roles in the provisional Texas governments of the Permanent Council, Consultation and General Council while also journeying to Washington-on-the-Brazos, where he signed the Texas Declaration of Independence of March 2, 1836. It was during this juncture that, according to Grimes's descendants, William B. Travis addressed to Jesse Grimes what is considered the most famous letter in Texas history, describing conditions at the Alamo.

Travis wrote to Grimes: "I am still here, in fine spirits and well to do, with 145 men I have held this place ten days against a force variously estimated from 1500 to 5000, and shall continue to hold it till I get relief from my countrymen or I will perish in its defense." He added that "under a flag of independence, we are ready to peril our lives a hundred times a day." It was only a few days later, on March 6, that the Alamo fell to the Mexican dictator Santa Anna.

After Texas won freedom at the Battle of San Jacinto on April 21, 1836, October of that year marked the first session of the congress of the Texas Republic. It was as senate president *pro tempore* that Jesse Grimes guided a bill through the senate to give the name Travis to a county that would come to stretch from the Brazos to the Trinity and from Spring Creek to the San

Antonio Road. The bill was destined to die on June 8, 1837, in a committee that Jesse Grimes, ironically, orchestrated, called the "Committee on County Boundaries." On December 14, 1837, the county projected to be called Travis assumed instead the name of Montgomery.

Upon playing a pivotal role in the county's founding, including nurturing a close friendship with then–Texas president Sam Houston, Jesse Grimes, trusted friend of William B. Travis, became the first chief justice of Montgomery County, while later Grimes County took his name.

Montgomery County was the third county created under the authority of the Republic of Texas, after Houston and Fannin Counties. At the session that named

Jesse Grimes. *Courtesy of Russell Cushman, blogspot.com.*

Montgomery County, on December 14, 1837, nine men from the county received appointments to look for a county seat, settling on the town of Montgomery by the next year, 1838. Those nine men were James Mitchell, Pleasant Gray, William Robinson, Elijah Collard, Charles Garrett, Joseph L. Bennett, B.B. Goodrich, D.D. Dunham and Henry Fanthorp.

CHAPTER 9

MONTGOMERY COUNTY

THE FORMATIVE YEARS

Montgomery County was created in 1837, and the reduction of its vast territory began in 1846, only nine years later, when it yielded land to form the counties of Grimes and Walker. Seven years later, Madison County came into existence, comprising territory that once was northern Montgomery County. In 1870, San Jacinto County made its appearance, with its western portion occupying what had until then been original Montgomery County territory. Finally, in 1873, a small portion of Montgomery County became part of Waller County.

As its borders were undergoing transformation, changes were also being wrought in the towns of the county. The town of Montgomery continued to be the county seat and hub of county activities through the Civil War. However, several other thriving communities challenged its preeminence before that war. Two of these communities, Huntsville and Cincinnati, became a part of Walker County, while "Old" Waverly joined San Jacinto County and "New" Waverly remained in Walker County. Another community, Anderson, became a part of Grimes County in 1846.

Danville remained in Montgomery County, while in the later nineteenth century, Willis challenged Montgomery's leadership for several decades before yielding to Conroe. Conroe became the county seat in 1889, encompassing the first fifty-two years of the county's existence.

MONTGOMERY

One of the great mysteries of the town of Montgomery centers on the elusive James Montgomery. He is even a possible namesake of the town. In 1923, Anna Davis, then sixteen and in high school, wrote a school paper based on a discussion with her grandmother, who quoted old-timers claiming the town was named for James Montgomery in 1830. Possible credence for this lies in the timeline: the grandmother would have been in direct contact with people from that era. Furthermore, the "Crittenden papers" of an old western Montgomery County family state that James Montgomery was buried in the Joel Greenwood Cemetery, a few miles north of Plantersville. (We will address this cemetery more later.) Furthermore, Anna was linked to the Landrums—William and his wife, Nancy Gilmore, and Zachariah and his wife, Letetia—who received land grants in the Montgomery area in 1831.

The year 1830 was also when another candidate for the namesake of the town appeared. Margaret Montgomery Shannon arrived in that year with her husband, Owen Shannon. Owen and Margaret married in Wilkes County, Georgia, on October 22, 1792. Owen was the son of Thomas and Eleanor Shannon. Both father and son had served in the American Revolution and received bounty land in Franklin County, Georgia, for their services. Owen and Margaret came to Pecan Point, off the Red River above Nacogdoches, in 1822, then moved to San Augustine and spent some time in the Atascocita District near Livingston before settling in Montgomery in 1830.

Another important family in the region was the Cartwrights. The patriarch was Peter Cartwright, who brought his family from Tennessee in 1831 and settled in an area called Bear Bend. This was in a region now known as Rayburn Chapel, a few miles southeast of Montgomery. Cartwright's daughter, Narcissa, became the third wife of J.G.W. Pierson. Pierson's second wife, Elizabeth Montgomery, died in 1833. Also part of this family were Matthew and William Cartwright, whose roles in the Texas Revolution were mentioned in the previous chapter.

Perhaps the most famous figure in relation to general Texas history to settle in Montgomery was Charles B. Stewart, mentioned in the last chapter as the first secretary of state in Texas and a signer of the Texas Declaration of Independence at Washington-on-the-Brazos. In addition, Stewart was a man of medicine and a dealer in real estate. In May 1997, Texas House Resolution 1123, signed by Governor George Bush, recognized Stewart—

and, by extension, Montgomery County—as the official "Birthplace of the Lone Star Flag" in 1839. Stewart also served several terms in the Texas legislature.

Another man of high stature was John Wade, mentioned earlier as a caretaker of the "twin sisters" cannons from Cincinnati during the Texas Revolution. In 1845, Wade began a newspaper called the *Montgomery Patriot*. The editor rejoiced over the establishment of a stage line to Houston with weekly trips "at the low rate for passengers of seven dollars each way."

Also in 1845, Montgomery established a Masonic lodge, including the following members: B. Gillespie, John Gillespie, L.G. Clepper, Milton Norton, Gwyn Morrison, Buford Oliphant, I.G. Sheppard, P.W. Bennett, W.B. Ochiltree, L.D. Hay, Charles Severn, Jesse Womack, A. Perry, I. Scott, Charles B. Stewart, W.W. Hawthorn, B.H. Halstead, John Womack and Sam Houston.

Sam Houston was a frequent visitor to Montgomery. On those occasions, he would usually stay at the Price Hotel under the ownership of Dr. Price, one of the two prominent physicians in Montgomery, the other being Dr. Arnold. During these stopovers, Houston made a fast friend of Stith Price, slave of Dr. Price. On those occasions, Stith received the assignment of sitting at Sam Houston's door until the wee hours, providing him candles as he read—Sam Houston was a light sleeper. On one occasion, Stith told of Houston weeping and stomping the floor upon reading of the death of Rachel Jackson, wife of President Andrew Jackson. Houston referenced her as "Aunt Rachel."

Another celebrity to make the news in old Montgomery was the theologian Rufus Burleson. En route to a meeting in Huntsville, Burleson took time to visit with Mrs. Aaron Shannon, a Baptist lady, who, in turn,

Statue at Baylor University of Rufus Burleson, twice president of that university. The statue was erected four years after his death. *Public domain.*

called in a few other ladies, including the wife of Dr. Arnold. Together they talked scripture until late. When Burleson finally convinced them that he must go, they invited him to take what they called a "nigh cut" through the forest, which would save six miles. That Burleson did, but, all being unaware that a tornado had recently devastated the route, he was detained mightily, suffering a near attack by wolves as he struggled through the mire. Ever after, he occasionally preached sermons on his Montgomery adventure and the folly of taking a "nigh cut" in life.

In 1848, Montgomery became incorporated, with Judge Nat Hart Davis as its first mayor. Judge Davis became one of the most distinguished citizens of early Texas and added greatly to Montgomery's fame as one of the most important trading centers of the state. On Montgomery's main street is a museum named for Judge Davis. A Texas marker in front makes a claim for the naming of Montgomery, this one surmising that W.W. Shepperd's newspaper ad in July 1837 selling lots in "Montgomery" marked the founding of the town at the site of his store.

DANVILLE

The communities that rivaled Montgomery before the Civil War were Danville, Waverly and Cincinnati. At its zenith, Danville supported a population of well over three hundred whites with some one thousand or so slaves. Two physicians, H.S. Hughes and W.L. Freeman, served the town, which at its height featured some fourteen businesses.

There was only one gin in downtown Danville, and it stood on the southwest corner of Main Street. Dr. Charles B. Stewart, the former statesman of Montgomery, operated the gin for a while with the assistance of W.D. Westmoreland. Among the many other important settlers around Danville were the Weisingers. The ancestors of this family in America were four German brothers who came over with the Hessian army to fight with the British during the Revolutionary War but who eventually joined the Americans.

A notable event in Danville's history came in 1858, when Sam Houston made there a famous speech, featuring his argument for the United States to make a protectorate of Mexico. His underpinning idea was a common task to keep the North and South together on the eve of the Civil War.

WAVERLY

Several miles east of Danville was the town of Waverly, the beginnings of which trace to the 1834 entrance into the area of the James Winters family, in the company of a family named Bankhead. Married to Rhoda Beal, James Winters and his bride had seven boys: William, Orin, John F.W., Benjamin Franklin, Elisha Willis, Billington Taylor and James W. We heard of three of these and their roles in the Texas Revolution in the previous chapter.

The Bankheads later moved to the San Jacinto River bottoms, some ten miles southwest of Huntsville. With them was George Lamb, who was, as mentioned earlier, the first to meet death in the Battle of San Jacinto, a second lieutenant in William Ware's Second Company.

Another early arrival about the time of the Winterses and Bankheads in the vicinity of Waverly was Richard Williams, mentioned earlier as a participant in the Texas Revolution. In 1836, Richard married Mary Miller, daughter of Ruthy Shannon and James Miller of Grimes Prairie. Ruthy Shannon Miller was the daughter of Owen Shannon and Margaret Montgomery Shannon of Montgomery.

The legend of Richard Williams lives, as in the immediate post–Civil War days he was suspected of the murder of three Union soldiers stationed in his area. The suspicion centered on the assumption that Williams buried them under his home, which left it haunted, or so the story goes.

Among a second group of settlers to enter Waverly were Colonel John Hill, Colonel H.M. Elmore and Colonel F.M. Lewis. Many of the homes of these settlers were built in the southern colonial style, with long front galleries and big rooms with high ceilings. Many literary conversations graced gatherings in these homes. It was after one of these conversations that Colonel F.M. Lewis obtained a consensus to name the community Waverly, after Sir Walter Scott's Waverly novels.

Waverly soon became a flourishing town with a population of around seven hundred. Its citizens gained a reputation far and wide as exemplars of finance, farming, education and culture. The citizenry even established an academy. Alas, as with Danville, the Civil War followed by the coming of the railroad led to the decline of Waverly, to be succeeded by a new town called New Waverly.

CINCINNATI

The third of the towns birthed in original Montgomery County and beginning with high promise, only to fall by the wayside due to the Civil War and the coming of the railroad, was Cincinnati. According to one source from the late 1800s, "old-timers claim that the site of Cincinnati, once queen city of the Trinity River's Steamboat trade, is now so deserted that even the ghosts have left forwarding addresses."

Cincinnati was located in the northeastern corner of the original Montgomery County, which Walker County absorbed. This once-thriving town was the hub of the shipping industry in East Texas, being one of the largest of the more than forty-six river ports that dotted the Trinity for four hundred miles through Texas. In its prime in 1853, it boasted thirty-nine city blocks, fourteen avenues and over 600 people. Not included in this count were the more than 1,200 farmers who resided on its periphery. Cincinnati had twenty or more stores and claimed to be the state's fastest-growing city.

The city's prosperity dwindled within a few months' time when a plague of yellow fever decimated the town in 1853. The cause traced to a stranger who stayed in an inn under the proprietorship of Captain George Hunter seeking to recover from an illness, which turned out to be yellow fever. The stranger left after a few days, only to die in Galveston within a week. Meanwhile, Mrs. Hunter and others who had tried to treat the stranger took ill, and thus yellow fever spread across the community. This plus the death of the steamboat trade, courtesy of the Union blockade in the Civil War, put an end to both the steamboat trade and the marvel that was Cincinnati, Texas.

HUNTSVILLE

Even as Cincinnati failed, Huntsville, a ways to the west, was thriving. Pleasant Gray, one of the nine men chosen at the assemblage that birthed original Montgomery County to search for a location for a county seat, settled there and named the town after Huntsville, Alabama. Gray first explored the then-future townsite in 1830 or 1831, camping near a spring just north of the present site of the post office. While exploring, he found Bidai Indians and, envisioning future lucrative trade with them, returned to Alabama to gather his family and bring them to the area.

Gray returned two or three years later, accompanied by his immediate family and his brother, Ephraim. On the northeast corner of the present courthouse square, Pleasant Gray built his home. Residing there, his wife, Hannah, had her fourth child, David, the first Anglo-American to be born in Huntsville. Near the site of the present courthouse, Gray built his trading post. On November 20, 1834, he wrote to the Mexican government of Coahuila and Texas, applying for land, which he received as a grant of seven square miles on July 10, 1835. Gray died in 1848 while on a prospecting tour to California.

When Walker County was created in 1846, Huntsville became its county seat. Historic sites abound in the city. Among them are the preserved homes of Sam Houston, the Sam Houston Memorial Museum and Sam Houston State University. Furthermore, the grave of that conqueror at San Jacinto is in Huntsville, as well as a huge statue of him at the Sam Houston Statue Visitor Center. In addition, Huntsville is the center of the state prison system.

MADISONVILLE

Another town from the original Montgomery County that has lived up to its potential is Madisonville. Located in the northern sector of the original county, Madisonville became the county seat of Madison County after that county's birth in 1853. Dr. Kitrell, as a representative of Walker County, petitioned the state legislature to form Madison County.

The two hundred acres of land on which the town of Madisonville emerged came from a donation courtesy of Job Stark Collard, a former resident of Danville and a veteran of the Battle of San Jacinto. Collard had received a Mexican land grant in the northern section of later Montgomery County in 1835, on which he settled in the early 1840s.

Job Collard came to Texas with his parents, Elijah and Mary Collard, sometime between 1832 and 1834. Four of their sons were named, respectively, Job Stark, Johnathan, James Harrison and Lemuel. All of these young men served Texas during the revolution. James conducted the first school at Montgomery in 1835 and was also one of the first licensed preachers in Texas.

One of the few other Anglo-Americans in the region at that time was James Mitchell, who had moved from Mitchell's Lake near Montgomery to reside east of Midway near Robbin's Ferry on the Trinity. Mitchell's location was northeast of Madisonville, at the divergence of the San Antonio and La Bahia Roads. Travelers bound for Bastrop, San Antonio and intermediate points followed the San Antonio Road, while those headed toward La Bahia, Gonzales or Goliad took the La Bahia. As more immigrants entered the area, Mitchell established a hotel at this strategic spot.

BEDIAS

Moving south from Madisonville, we come to the town of Bedias, named for the Bidai Indians. The first settler of note in the area of the town was Thomas Phiney Plaster, who established a plantation in 1835. For some time, the site was called Plasterville. Plaster participated in the Battle of San Jacinto, manning one of the "twin sisters" cannons. When Texas attained statehood, he became a representative.

The most prominent citizen of Bedias, historically, was Sarah Bradley Dodson, designer of an early Texas flag. While living in Harrisburg with her husband, Archelaus Dodson, a member of Captain Andrew Robinson's company, she designed a flag for the company, consisting of a white star set in a blue field in perpendicular mode adjoining in order a white and red field. The flag flew with the company in San Antonio at the Battles of Concepción and at the Siege of Bexar. It also was on display on March 1, 1836, at the opening of the Independence Convention at Washington-on-the-Brazos. Sarah Dodson is buried near Bedias in the Bethel Cemetery. Her flag is the official flag of Grimes County.

ROANS PRAIRIE

A few miles below Bedias, we come to Roans Prairie, at the intersection of Highways 90 and 30. The town took its name from Willis Roan. Appearing in 1841, he came to be the first to start a store, laying the groundwork for a community. By 1849, he was the community's first postmaster, giving the town its name.

Earlier, just south of town, on May 7, 1831, Joshua Hadley and his first wife, Obedience Grantham, and family received a league of land at the head of Rocky Creek, where he established a nice home and quarters known in the area as "Hadley's Fort" at "Hadley's Prairie." After the death of Obedience in 1839, he married Joyce Floyd in 1840. Josh Hadley, as mentioned in the last chapter, was the alcalde of Washington Municipality in 1835. He had previously represented the District of Viesca in the Texas Convention of

1832. Near Hadley, as mentioned in our earlier story of Mrs. Taylor, lived for a time Lieutenant Colonel Joseph L. Bennett, of fame in the Battle of San Jacinto and other events in the history of Montgomery County.

ANDERSON

Moving south from Roans Prairie, there was the community of Anderson. Its history begins with a pioneer named Andrew Millican, who settled some three and one-half miles west of present Anderson, off what came to be called Ten Mile Creek. After one season, he left his log cabin to search north, finding a place that came to be named for him: Millican. While Andrew Millican was away on that initial foray, the families of two brothers, Francis and William Holland, along with a friend, William Burney, happened along to temporarily occupy the Millican cabin. When Millican returned, he allowed them to stay.

Francis Holland received the title to Millican's property in 1826. William Holland and William Burney filed claims nearby. Soon others came in, including a sister of the Holland brothers, Mrs. Mary Peterson, who was a medical doctor, and the families of John and Wesley Fisher.

Francis Holland and his wife had four sons and two daughters: Tapley, who died at the Alamo; Susan, Nancy, James, Francis and William. Tragically, every Holland by name of the Francis Holland line died within two years of each other. First William; then his father, Francis; then his mother; then Tapley, at the Alamo; then James; then Francis the younger.

In 1833, Henry Fanthorp, from England, purchased the eastern quarter of the Francis Holland property. He developed first a corn storage facility, then—after broadening the house—a stage line stop, an inn and finally, in 1835, a post office, giving the site and surrounding community the name of Fanthorp. In 1846, the last vice president of the Texas Republic, Kenneth Lewis Anderson, died at the inn just after laying the groundwork for Texas to become a state. Hence the name of Anderson for the community, absorbing both the names Fanthorp and an earlier name, Alta Mira ("high view"). Along the way, Henry Fanthorp married Rachel Kennard, of the nearby A.D. Kennard family. Rachel's brother, Mike Kennard, and Abraham Womack partnered with Henry Fanthorp on several business ventures. The marriage of Henry and Rachel was the first marriage in the western sector of the original Montgomery County. Performing the ceremony was Reverend Daniel Parker, of the famous

Parker Clan associated with Fort Parker. Daniel, as mentioned earlier, chaired the committee that formed the Texas Rangers.

Another famous Texian of the era living in Anderson was Dr. Benjamin Briggs Goodrich. This was the same B.B. Goodrich whom we addressed earlier as a signer of the Texas Declaration of Independence and whose brother, John G. Goodrich, died in the Alamo. As mentioned in the previous chapter, Patrick Jack was also a citizen of early Anderson.

NAVASOTA

Ten miles west of Anderson lies the town of Navasota. It is named for the Navasota River, which is linked to an encounter on its banks in the 1540s between Indians and a Spanish expedition led initially by Hernando de Soto. Indians believed that the spirits of the dead were associated with rivers. Accordingly, though de Soto had died and been interred earlier in the Mississippi River, the remaining components of his expedition made it to Navasota where, it is said, they took advantage of an aspect of the American Indian lore. They manipulated the Indians to envision de Soto's spirit as reborn in their river, hence the legendary term "Nativity de Soto" (birth of de Soto), shortened to Navasota.

Navasota historically has revolved around the theme of rebirth, as the concept of the "Cradle of Texas Road," mentioned earlier, stems from the death of La Salle near later Navasota, which led to Father Damián Massanet and Alonso de León journeying to East Texas near later Alto to establish Mission San Francisco de las Tejas. The word *tejas*—or *tayshas* in the Caddo language—was the word for friends among the Caddo tribe, to whom the Spanish were ministering. The translation of *tejas* to English is Texas.

Building on the story of Francis Holland, which led to Anderson's beginning, the area associated with the Francis Holland grant is also linked to Navasota, as Hollandale stretched from Ten Mile Creek into near Navasota proper. Then in 1832, Daniel Arnold and Daniel Tyler received grants in the area through Stephen Austin's "Old Three Hundred," the name for members of his first colony.

Things began to pick up toward the birth of a real town when James Nolan came to town, complete with his pet bear. Nolan first set up tents, then a log cabin and, by the early 1850s, a stage line that quickly served as a model for four stage lines. It was in 1854 that the town officially assumed the name of Navasota.

"Judge" James Nolan left as his legacy the title of "Father of Navasota," as he played a pivotal role in generating a thriving community at the crossroads of the old Bahia Road and, on some maps, the lower Coushatta trace. That Indian trail reached eastward to near Montgomery and beyond to the Coushatta headquarters on the Trinity and westward to Washington-on-the-Brazos. Among his actions, Nolan established a blacksmith shop, where, on the side, he sponsored bets on who could win a wrestling match with his pet bear.

Among other historic sites in Navasota are the ruins of the old Camp Hotel and Stagecoach Inn. Ira Malcolm Camp established his business just to the east of present Navasota. From rocks in his fields, he built an imposing structure, cementing it together with lime imported from Italy. There was also a cellar, the entrance to which was kept covered by a rug. Sam Houston was known to stay there on occasion.

Historic sites in Navasota include two statues of La Salle. One of these is on the main street, Washington Avenue, while the other is in the Navasota Park across from the VFW Hall off Highway 105 West. Downtown is a statue of the famous African American blues singer Mance Lipscomb and, on the courthouse square, a Russell Cushman–made statue of Frank Hamer, famous marshal of Navasota and later the brains behind the final demise of the dynamic robber duo of Bonnie and Clyde.

GRIMES PRAIRIE

Leaving Navasota and traveling east on Highway 105, we come to Grimes Prairie, home of Jesse Grimes, a pivotal figure. Let's explore his remarkable life and career. He is the man for whom Grimes County was named and a central figure in the general history of Montgomery County and, indeed, the state of Texas. From his birth in Duplin County, North Carolina, on February 6, 1788, through his service in the War of 1812, through his time living in Alabama and then on to Texas, Jesse Grimes lived a life of adventure and of high service to humankind.

Upon the death of his first wife, Martha Smith, Grimes married Rosanna Ward. Together, these hearty pioneer women presented him with fifteen children. One of these children, Charles Grimes, became a martyr to the cause of Texas's independence at the Alamo in March 1836. In 1827, with Rosanna, Jesse Grimes settled in what would become known as Grimes Prairie in the western portion of the original Montgomery County, now in Grimes County.

Dangerous were conditions in Grimes Prairie while Jesse and Rosanna were raising their family there—so much so that on the occasions, and there were many, when Jesse ventured away from home, a Bidai Indian friend of his would stand guard around the Grimes home. Jesse was a friend to the various tribes who inhabited the region or traveled through frequently, visiting and counseling with them on numerous occasions.

The people of the general area held much faith in Jesse Grimes. This is evidenced in the numerous offices that he assumed. From 1821 to 1836, Mexico ruled Texas. In 1830, Mexican authorities marked off a vast area stretching from the Brazos to near the Trinity River and named the region the District of Viesca. Within this grand expanse of territory, in two years' time, Jesse became, in turn, a lieutenant of militia; a *sindico procurador*, similar to a municipal attorney; a regidor, or councilman; and treasurer of the district.

In 1835, Jesse became a regidor of Washington Municipality, serving under Joshua Hadley as alcalde. Later in 1835, he became a member of the provisional government. Then, in the face of hostile Mexican forces, on March 2, 1836, brave men gathered at Washington-on-the-Brazos. Jesse Grimes was there, representing Washington Municipality. He was among those who signed the Texas Declaration of Independence. Texas stood as a republic from 1836 until February 1846. During that time, Jesse became the first chief justice of Montgomery County and served four terms representing Montgomery County in the legislature.

A year after Texas succeeded to statehood, in 1846, out of the western portion of Montgomery County Grimes County was born. For four terms, Jesse Grimes was state senator from Grimes County, even serving for a time as president *pro tempore* of the senate.

Jesse Grimes died on March 15, 1866, a pioneer and patriarch of two counties.

ORIGINAL MONTGOMERYS OF MONTGOMERY COUNTY

A near friend to Jesse Grimes was Andrew Montgomery. There are several indications of this friendship. For starters, in 1855, Grimes—along with Dr. B.B. Goodrich of Anderson, a signer of the Texas Declaration of Independence, and Gwyn Morrison, chief justice of Montgomery County—was witness to a legal document legitimizing Andrew's request for support based on his service to Texas. In the document, they gave credence to his claim to have been on expeditions to Texas, as Andrew put it, "*at least* as early as 1820." Parenthetically, it was also in 1820 that Moses Austin ventured into Andrew's base in the Pecan Point area to visit his son, Stephen, as a prelude to Moses's trip to Texas.

This Andrew document lends some credence to the claims of Andrew's son, Baily Montgomery, that Andrew served with the James Long expedition of 1819–21. In 1819, from Nacogdoches, Long's forces worked the area around Pecan Point off the Red River associated with Andrew's family.

Another indication of close relations between Andrew and Jesse Grimes lies in the site of Andrew's home, on one of his official land grants, this one in Stoneham near Grimes Prairie and Grimes Road. Furthermore, in late spring 1836—after Andrew, with his brother John, had fought at the Battle of San Jacinto in April—he and Jesse were named together in several sources as giving special assistance to the Parkers in the aftermath of the Fort Parker massacre.

All of Andrew's siblings and his father, William Montgomery, lived in the original Montgomery County area beginning in the early 1820s. Grants in the area between Grimes Prairie and Montgomery, most as early as 1831, went to his brothers, Edley and John Montgomery, and to his sisters, Mary Jane and Anna Montgomery, as wives of the Greenwood brothers, Franklin and Joel. Additionally, his father, William, held an 1831 grant and land centering on present Plantersville, on which he lived with his youngest child, Sarah Montgomery. The remaining sister, Elizabeth Montgomery, second wife of J.G.W. Pierson, is said to be buried in the Joel Greenwood Cemetery, a few miles north of Plantersville.

In late 1833 or early 1834, Andrew, Edley and John followed Pierson to Robertson's Colony above the San Antonio Road as chief assistants to Sterling Robertson, the head of the colony. All of these men came to hold grants in the colony, Andrew being the surveyor for the grant of Robertson himself. In February 1836, with Robertson in Mexico, James W. Robinson, acting president of Texas at the time, appointed Pierson acting head of the colony to organize support in the area for the impending Texas Revolution. In Robinson's message to Pierson, he noted that many of the colonists were from "Montgomery and Grimes Prairie," a source of primary evidence that Montgomery received its name before 1837, countering arguments elsewhere. John Montgomery was constable of Viesca Precinct in 1837.

Along with James Montgomery and Margaret Montgomery Shannon, mentioned earlier, Andrew and William are possible namesakes of the town of Montgomery and the original county.

HOW CONROE BECAME THE COUNTY SEAT

Conroe's emergence as the county seat of Montgomery County marked the final installment of a three-act drama centered on the coming of the railroads.

Our story begins in the year 1837. That was the year Montgomery County became the third county created under the authority of the Republic of Texas. Shortly after this event, the town of Montgomery became the county seat. Two of the earliest and most respected citizens of the town were the brothers Peter and Richard Willis. The brothers found wives and settled into a lucrative mercantile business. As time went on, they began searching for adventure beyond the bounds of their beloved Montgomery. Their search led them to purchase a block of land to the east known as Mockingbird Hill. This purchase set the stage for our three-part drama.

Act one of the drama came after the Willis brothers donated Mockingbird Hill to the forerunner of the International and Great Northern Railroad. When the railroad extended through the site, the site quickly became the location of the town of Willis. Willis emerged in 1872. Just two years later, the town that the Willis brothers helped spawn issued a challenge to unseat Montgomery as the county seat. In the resultant election, the vote was 788 to 646 in favor of Willis. Since this was short of the two-thirds margin needed to declare victory, the next six years were spent in a matrix of confusion over which city was actually in charge of the county's political business.

In 1880, act two of the railroad drama decided the issue after the Central and Montgomery Railway completed a branch line from Navasota to Montgomery. In an election that year, Montgomery received 1,308 votes to Willis's 1,243, confirming the former as the county seat.

The impact of the railroad industry on Montgomery County politics was not to end there, however, for act three was soon to follow. In 1881, Isaac Conroe moved the headquarters of his sawmill some two miles west of its previous location on Stewart Creek, a move that placed him strategically close to the International and Great Northern line that ran north and south.

By the mid-'80s, near the site was established a post office called Conroe's Switch, named after Isaac, its postmaster. Shortly thereafter, intersecting the site from the west was the Gulf, Colorado and Santa Fe Rail Line. In 1889, Conroe's Switch, by then known simply as Conroe, won the right to become the county seat in place of Montgomery by sixty-two votes.

Thus did the curtain fall on act three of the drama.

CHAPTER 10

THREE PIONEER PREACHERS

Z.N. Morrell: A Pioneer Preacher's "Lesson of the Rattlesnake"

One of the most colorful preachers in the Texas Republic was Z.N. Morrell. In 1844, he wrote: "My mind was impressed strongly that my labors were in demand in the county of Montgomery." Though his mark on our county was significant, his most memorable adventure stemmed from an earlier encounter with rattlesnakes when he was, as he put it, "west of Brazos."

In 1838, with a group of surveyors, Morrell ventured on horseback to the coastal area near Corpus Christi. On one occasion, he and a companion named Matthew Burnett broke off from the group for a little private reconnoitering of the area. Soon they saw in the distance a fine-looking wild cow. Their appetites thus whetted for beef, the men prepared their guns to fell the beast.

Just as Matthew Burnett was about to fire, Morrell spotted a horse striding slowly toward the cow. Then, just ahead of the horse, he spotted an Indian youth crawling in high weeds, with bow and arrow poised to strike the cow. Burnett, also spotting the Indian, turned his weapon to fire at him.

Quickly, Morrell commanded Burnett not to fire. The reason: Morrell remembered the lesson he had recently learned from rattlesnakes. Meandering through a brush pile, Morrell and others had disturbed two huge and beautiful snakes. Instead of immediately striking the men, the serpents reared their noble heads and, with their rattlers, sounded a warning. This allowed the men time to plan an attack and prevail in the ensuing battle. Still, it impressed Morrell that the snakes had fought only in self-defense.

It was remembrance of this scene that gave Morrell pause in the case of the Indian youth. The preacher explained that the Indian was doing them no harm, hence there was no need to engage in a battle of self-defense. Therefore, the men left the potentially tasty spot of beef to the Indian.

Hungry, yet satisfied that they had done the right thing, they returned to their companions. Suddenly, a band of Karankawa Indians appeared, prompting the men to go for their weapons. However, to their great surprise, the Karankawa leader gave a sign of peace.

Puzzled that a group of Indians known for their prowess at tying victims to a stake and eating their flesh right before their eyes would seek a peaceful meeting, Morrell and company sought an answer. It turned out to be very simple: the youth whom Morrell had refused to shoot was the chief's son. On the spot, Morrell and company made a treaty of peace with the Karankawa that received official sanction from Sam Houston.

Ever after, Morrell would often intersperse sermons with the "Lesson of the Rattlesnake."

James W. Parker: Hero or Villain?

The Parkers, sojourners in original Montgomery County, were an intriguing and innovative family. Especially intriguing were three of the brothers, Daniel, Silas and James. Daniel—like James, a preacher—chaired the committee at the Consultation that, on October 17, 1835, launched the Texas Rangers. Both Silas and James became rangers. Against this background, let's explore the enigmatic life of James W. Parker.

James and Silas left their homes off what is now Highway 105 between Navasota and Montgomery, an area in original Montgomery County during the time of our story, to set up a fort appropriately named Fort Parker in present Limestone County, Texas. Here, on May 19, 1836, Comanches attacked the fort, killing Silas, among others, while taking into captivity Silas's daughter, Cynthia Ann, and son, John, along with James's daughter, Rachel Plummer, and her son, James Pratt, in addition to Elizabeth Kellogg. This marked the beginning of the march to fame and infamy for James W. Parker.

Disgusted with his son-in-law, Luther, husband of Rachel Plummer, for refusing to join him, over the course of nine years Parker set off alone on several harrowing trips, seeking his daughter and grandson, as well as his niece and nephew. Along the way, others rescued his daughter, Rachel, along with his niece and nephew, while he finally procured his grandson, James Pratt, at which point his ambivalent son-in-law refused to help reimburse him for his efforts and sacrifices. Accordingly, Sam Houston, by then president of the Texas Republic and probably unaware of the full depth of the story, wrote a scathing letter to James W., demanding that he deliver the boy to his father.

Meanwhile, indicative of his sacrifices, James had rescued seventeen survivors of the massacre and guided them through several hundred miles of dangerous travel to their original Montgomery County base, before returning to bury the dead at the fort. As documented in *The Rachel Plummer Narrative* and other sources, Andrew Montgomery and Jesse Grimes—later first chief justice of Montgomery County, a senator and namesake of Grimes County—arranged shelter for the group.

After all his efforts, James Parker suffered much criticism. One particularly repulsive scene took place in old Montgomery in 1838. Even as Parker sat astride his horse on a public street, a proprietor of a local store, W.W. Shepperd, publicly rebuked him with accusations of conspiring with the Comanches at Fort Parker to the point of giving them counterfeit money, resulting in the attack on Parker's own family. That family included not only his brother and children, but also his aged father!

Shepperd's accusations lose credibility in light of similar published diatribes of his against such prominent citizens as Jared Groce, close friend of Sam Houston and owner of Groce's Retreat, where the Texas Declaration of Independence was written on the evening of March 1, 1836.

Thus does James Parker's legacy rest on these and other shadowy charges, never proven in court, intermixed with proven exploits of bravery and persistence, at great sacrifice.

REVEREND MOSES SPEER

On January 27, 1995, the *United Methodist Reporter* ran a column entitled "Historical Group Marks Grave of Moses Speer." Speer met his death on July 11, 1840, in the Robinson Settlement (Martha's Chapel) area, southwest of Huntsville. Born in 1768 in Maryland, Speer was reared in Kentucky. In 1793, he joined the Kentucky Methodist Conference, and by 1804 he was preaching in the Cumberland Circuit around Nashville, Tennessee. By the late 1830s, he was assigned to the Montgomery County, Texas District, where he ranged from Montgomery to Huntsville. Let's examine the perilous times through which Moses Speer engaged his early ministry.

At the end of the French and Indian War in 1763, the King of England declared the territory between the Appalachians and the Mississippi River to be Indian Territory. However, by 1771, fires of revolution were kindling east of the Appalachians. In that year, restless under British rule, a group led by James Robertson, destined to receive the title of "Father of Tennessee," crossed over Appalachia to establish a colony named Watauga in the Cumberland and Holston area of western North Carolina.

Four years later, a group—which included Daniel Boone as guide—purchased twenty million acres bordered by the Kentucky River on the north, the Ohio on the west and the Cumberland on the south and east. Called Transylvania, the area included much of later southern Kentucky and northern Tennessee. In reaction, Dragging Canoe, son of the pacifist Cherokee chief Attakullakulla, ignited the Chickamauga War, which ranged over most of the territory between the Appalachians and the Mississippi River. The war lasted until 1794, overlapping the U.S. Revolutionary War, which saw Dragging Canoe side with the British.

The 1783 treaties between Spain and Britain on the one hand and Britain and the United States on the other left in dispute ownership of the Mississippi River and the boundary of Spanish Florida. By 1784, Spain formally claimed the Mississippi and an area including much of Transylvania. By then James Robertson and others had established Nashville, capital of an area called the Cumberland District. Great was the intrigue as the Americans in this vast area played the fledgling American government against the Spanish, even as the area fell victim to vicious Indian attacks. James Robertson, for example, lost two brothers and three sons to Indian warfare.

Meanwhile, by 1780 James Robertson and others had formed in Nashville the famous Cumberland Pact, which would come to include in its leadership John Montgomery, namesake of later Montgomery County, Tennessee, as sheriff and Andrew Jackson as the group's attorney. Serving as secretary of the group was Andrew Ewing. Besides keeping meticulous records over many years, Ewing played a vital role as "Plenipotentiary to the Creek Nation" at the height of the Indian Wars.

It was a daughter of Andrew Ewing, Amelia, whom Moses Speer wed to become a member of the establishment of Nashville. During this time, Methodism was beginning to catch on in the area, and Amelia became part of the early practitioners of that denomination. Building on strong family connections, Moses Speer, even while manning a sawmill, became a key player in building the ministry of Methodism in Tennessee. Later he continued through the Red River country on to San Augustine and Jasper, Texas, before ending his career and his life in Robinson's Settlement, now called Martha's Chapel. A Christian pioneer of the first order was Moses Speer.

HAVING SURVEYED THE HISTORY and events relating to the Cradle of Texas Road before, during and immediately after the era of the Texas Republic, we now turn to Part II to address events and items surrounding the Texas connection to Manifest Destiny.

PART II

THE SPIRIT OF MANIFEST DESTINY

IMPACT ON THE CRADLE OF TEXAS ROAD

CHAPTER 11

THE LEGACY
OF MANIFEST DESTINY № 1

EDUCATING THE MIND

Giving vent to what John O'Sullivan would label Manifest Destiny in 1845, Stephen F. Austin sought early on to build a foundation for Anglo-style democracy in Texas through his education policy. As will be shown, over time, realities of race and cultural differences modified, to an extent, his idealism. Accordingly, in this chapter we will explore the framework of educational policy as reflected in the Anglo-Texan mind, including examples of education in specific arenas of our area of reference.

We begin with a portrayal of the significance of education to the second president of the Republic of Texas, Mirabeau B. Lamar, who has been called the "Father of Education in Texas." In December 1838, President Lamar addressed the Congress of the Republic. In that address, he made explicit the importance of education to the grounding of a viable political culture:

> If we desire to establish a Republican Government upon a broad and permanent basis, it will be our duty to adopt a comprehensive and well-regulated system of mental and moral culture....It is admitted by all, that a cultivated mind is the guardian genius of democracy, and while guided and controlled by virtue, is the noblest attribute of man. It is the only dictator that free men desire....Our young Republic has been formed by a Spartan Spirit. Let it progress and ripen into Roman firmness, and Athenian gracefulness....Let me therefore urge it upon you, gentlemen, not to postpone the matter too long. The present is a propitious moment to lay the foundation of the moral and intellectual edifice, which will in after ages be hailed as the chief ornament and blessing of Texas.

If Mirabeau Lamar is the Father of Education in Texas, Stephen F. Austin must be Texas Education's Grandfather. For without the foundation that Austin laid, Lamar and the republic and later state would be standing on less solid ground. Austin was riding the crest of a pivotal era in the history of ideas. The vanguard of the American settlers in Texas were Scotch-Irish immigrants who, prior to the American Revolutionary War, lived along the eastern edge of the Appalachian Mountains. The Blue Ridge, which formed the backbone of that mountain range, had proved a formidable barrier to westward expansion during the American colonial era, but upon the signing of the Treaty of Paris in 1783, those hearty independent pioneers spilled through its passes into the fertile Mississippi Valley. The forefathers of the pioneers to Texas had left Europe to escape the traditional class distinction that infringed upon their rights and privileges. Nevertheless, during the many years that England governed the colonists, the English social order prevailed in those colonies.

The English social order centered on a double-track system of education. There was a leadership class and a class of, essentially, followers. What academic training the followers or lower-class individuals received was confined to people's schools. The colonists brought the people's schools from Europe to train the farmers and workers, while an imitation of the European secondary school and the English college would impart quality education to the wealthier few. Coinciding with the emergence of Austin's Colony, the old European double-track system was in a process of decay among the American colonists.

Stephen Austin assumed the goal of implementing a quality education on as broad a level as possible. The environment in Texas in which he engaged in his task was pregnant with limitations. Among those limitations was the great distance between the early settlements, without a viable system of roads connecting them. Then there was the ever-present threat of Indian depredations and the basic apathy of the Mexican government to the cause of education. Finally, there was a dearth of qualified teachers. Austin sought to compensate for these difficulties by admitting to his colony people of quality. This is exemplified in Austin's written requirements for entering his colony as a permanent resident:

No one will be received as a Settler, or even be permitted to remain in the country longer than is absolutely necessary to prepare for a removal who does not produce the most unequivocal and satisfactory evidence of unblemished character, good Morals, Sobriety, and industrious habits, and he must also have sufficient property to begin with either as a farmer or mechanic besides paying for his land—No frontiersman who has no occupation than that of a hunter will be received—no drunkard, nor Gambler, nor profane swearer, idler, nor any man against whom there is even probable grounds of suspicion that he is a bad man, or even has been considered a bad or disorderly man will be received. Those who are rejected on the grounds of bad character will be immediately ordered out of the Country and if the order is not obeyed, they will be sent off under guard and their property seized and sold to pay the expenses, and should forcible resistance be made by them, the guard will be ordered to fire on and kill them.

Stephen F. Austin hoped that the Mexican government would provide the means for the quality colonists he recruited to develop a viable cultural framework for democracy. As a first step, in 1823, he recommended to the Mexican authorities a model of a liberal constitution. In Article 25, he set forth the fundamental purpose of the new government as the establishment of "a general system of education to appropriate the public funds…for the endowment and support of schools, academies and colleges or other literary institutions."

In Articles 26 and 27, Austin elaborated on the philosophical premises behind his proposed constitution:

Despotic Governments have endeavored to keep the minds of the people in darkness by prohibiting the introduction of books prescribed for their liberal principles. Free Governments on the contrary have thrown open the door for the admission of all without exception and experience has fully proved the beneficial effect of this liberal policy enlightening the people, who, very soon discriminate between any evil, irreligious or immoral doctrines which such books may contain, and the pure and virtuous ones, rejecting the former, and profiting by the latter. All restrictions or prohibitions therefore on the introduction, sale or reading of books, are calculated to prevent the diffusion of intellectual light, and knowledge: to retard the improvement of the nation, by perpetuating ignorance, Superstition and servile principles, and are at variance with the genius of free institutions and shall never be imposed under any pretext whatever.

A nation can only be free, happy and great in proportion to the virtue and intelligence of the people, the dissemination of useful knowledge and of the arts and sciences is therefore of primary importance to national liberty and prosperity, and to affect his great object, it shall be the duty of Congress

Stephen F. Austin. *Public domain.*

to provide by every means in their power for the speedy establishment of Schools, and academies and colleges throughout the whole nation for the instruction of youth and children.

There is evidence that Austin had an impact on the thinking of the Mexican government. This is seen in the establishment of the federal constitution in 1824 of Coahuila and Texas. Articles 215 and 217 of that state's constitution addressed public education:

In all the towns of the state a suitable number of primary schools shall be established, wherein shall be taught reading, writing, arithmetic, the catechism of the Christian religion, a brief and simple explanation of this constitution, and that of the republic, the rights and duties of man in society, and whatever else may conduce to the better education of youth. The method of teaching shall be uniform throughout the state, and with this view, also to facilitate the same, congress shall form a general plan of public education, and regulate by means of statutes and laws all that pertains to this most important subject.

Realizing that a primary underpinning for a common culture lay in a common language, Stephen Austin worked to integrate Mexican and Texan culture through the formation of an academy focusing on training in the Spanish language. In spite of Austin's efforts, the Mexican government failed to establish a viable educational system during the days of colonial Texas. This is evidenced in an excerpt from the Texas Declaration of Independence of March 2:

> [The government of Mexico] *has failed to establish any public system of education although possessed of almost boundless resources (of the public domain), and although it is an axiom in political science that, unless a people are educated and enlightened it is idle to expect continuance of civil liberty, or the capacity for self-government.*

Devoid of feasible support from the Mexican government, the Anglo-Texians themselves met some success in implementing an educational system. One of these measures of success Austin personally instigated, as revealed in a letter that he wrote to Josiah H. Bell dated February 24, 1829:

> *Mr. Pilgrim proposes to teach school. I am pleased with him so far as I have been able to judge....This subject is a very important one, it has always been a favorite one with me, and I think an effort should be now made to get the school under way, it can be added to afterwards—in fact it will naturally increase as its reputation becomes known and I fear that if the present opportunity passes of getting a permanent teacher another may not offer soon.*

By 1831, there were four schools in San Felipe, with seventy-seven students enrolled. Meanwhile, in the area of our Cradle Road, educational institutions were also developing. We will now survey examples of educational efforts in that region.

MONTGOMERY

In her unpublished paper on the "History of Montgomery," Mary Davis stated, "There is no record of the earliest schools, but from the beginning, the citizens seem to have realized the supreme importance of good schools, and to have planned for them." The first school at Montgomery was established in 1835. Its teacher was James Collard, the first young man to be licensed to preach in Texas.

In 1839, a German, Gustave Dresel, visited Montgomery and left elucidating remarks about the educational culture of the area compared to his native land:

> There were approximately ten farmers living in and about Montgomery Prairie. They united in keeping a teacher who boarded with one farmer this week, with the other next week. This custom is found wherever Americans live, even in the most distant woods. The education of the young is their first concern. By talent and knowledge every Republican may attain the highest honors of the state. Scholars are not to be met with as frequently as with us, to be sure. Neither do Americans look to scholarship as an ultimate object and on life merely as a means toward acquiring it, but in practical general knowledge they are superior to us. Americans live rather on solid ground while with us the whole population is hovering in the higher regions.

Informative of further cultural contrasts is the same Dresel's observations of a Christmas party in the Montgomery area, in this case four miles northwest of the county seat. Dresel wrote that "he did not want to do as the citizens of Montgomery and wallow on the buffalo skins, sunk in melancholic recoveries, while all Germany, jubilating, dancing, drinking, and kissing, rejoiced at having safely got over another year at finding everything as it had been before."

Consequently, on this Christmas Day, Dresel mounted his horse and galloped with determination some four miles to the county seat, bent on obtaining liquid spirits. Obtain them he did, four jugs full. Upon returning to the hinterlands, he recruited several of his new friends and proceeded to prowl the neighborhood. The Texians, he reported with admiration, "responded with enthusiasm to the jolly mood."

A particularly interesting interlude in this evening of spreading goodwill came in the home of Colonel Joseph L. Bennett, lately of fame as an officer of great courage at the pivotal battle for Texas Independence from Mexico at San Jacinto. Bennett's daughter baked a maize cake during the Yuletide gathering at her father's house. Upon taking "a draught to the welfare of the ladies," Dresel wrote, "we declared to the Colonel that we should neither budge nor withdraw until the last drop had wetted our lips." To Dresel's entreaty, Bennett replied, "In that case…let us brew an eggnog, that the ladies will not despise either."

So impressed was the German Dresel with the quick change of behavior of his hosts that he opined, "Whenever it is a matter of organizing a frolic, a spree, the Texians are not found wanting." Dresel's portrayal of that Christmas night in 1839 leaves us with unique insight into one sophisticated German's perception of the pioneers of old Montgomery.

In 1848, as we've seen, Montgomery became officially incorporated, with Judge Nat Hart Davis as its first mayor. Along with Baptist and Methodist churches and the fine Price Hotel, Montgomery was the home of Montgomery Academy during its antebellum days.

HIGH POINT

Let's again review this community founded by J.G.W. Pierson and his Montgomery family in-laws, which occupied an area near present Stoneham: G.W. Crittenden states that there was a school near the present Stoneham cemetery as early as 1834 and that there were three different teachers at work there over a short time. These were Allen Larrison, Joseph L. Bennett and James W. Parker. Larrison and Bennett were in the Battle of San Jacinto, Larrison a private and Bennett destined to be a lieutenant colonel at San Jacinto. Among other things, the irrepressible James W. Parker, as we've seen, was an itinerant preacher.

CINCINNATI

During the antebellum days, there were some forty-six river ports dotting the Trinity for four hundred miles upstream from the coast. The largest of these, once the hub of the shipping industry in Texas, was Cincinnati. Not only was it conveniently located off the Trinity but it was also on the main stage line from Nacogdoches to Washington-on-the-Brazos. A veteran of the Battle of San Jacinto, James De Witt, founded the town in 1838. Among the many marks of high civilization within its environs was the Cincinnati Classical and Collegiate Institute.

HUNTSVILLE

By 1844, in operation in Huntsville was the Huntsville Male and Female Academy. Also known as the Brick Academy, the school received its charter on April 11. Meanwhile, in the fall of 1845, Stovall's Male and Female Academy began operation. On March 16, 1848, the latter institution restricted its enrollment to males, becoming known, appropriately enough, as the Huntsville Male Institute. Subsequently, the Brick Academy came to cater exclusively to females. In the 1850s, the Methodist Church established Andrew Female College, while Austin College also began offering courses in Huntsville.

KENNARD'S PRAIRIE

A.D. Kennard and his wife, Sarah, and their seven children settled south of present Roans Prairie in 1832. The Kennard home was built originally in the form of a Tennessee blockhouse for protection against the Indians. Mr. Kennard and a few neighbors hired Samuel Millett to teach school on the premises. Born in Missouri in 1792, Mr. Millett brought four sons and one daughter to Austin's Colony in 1831. He later fought at the Battle of San Jacinto.

One of the students at the Kennard school was William Zuber. Zuber spoke of using candles made of beef tallow. Courses employed during this era included English grammar and geography. Books used were John Walker's *Dictionary*, Lindley Murray's *English Grammar* and John Adam's *Geography*.

ANDERSON

This county seat of Grimes County supported at least two academic institutions in the antebellum era. The first of these, which the Masons established in 1846, was known alternately as Masonic Collegiate Institute and Patrick Academy. The second school was St. Paul's Episcopal College, opened in 1852.

We turn next to addressing problems of cultural mix that impacted efforts toward education in our region of study.

CHAPTER 12

THE LEGACY OF MANIFEST DESTINY № 2

CLASH AND BLENDING OF THREE CULTURES: ANGLOS, TEJANOS AND INDIANS

Even as Stephen Austin worked diligently to mold a common base through education for a blending of the cultures of Texas, uncomfortable realities continued apace. The Tejanos whom Spain placed in charge of policing Texas were basically of mixed Spanish and Indian blood. Relations between Tejanos and mother Spain in the interior of Mexico were mixed. The main task of the Tejano lay in protecting the frontier. Feeling chagrined by the Mexican establishment, Tejanos came to sense ostensible advantages in welcoming in the Anglo-Americans and managed to offer them favorable terms. However, as the movement toward rebellion against mother Mexico broadened, problems arose. These and problems with Indians will be addressed in this chapter.

Tejanos were ambivalent during the drive for Texas independence. Their stances ranged from pro-Texas to ambivalent to neutral. The most dramatic effect conditioning Tejano-Texian relations was the Battle of the Alamo in March 1836. While there were Tejanos among the martyrs, before the battle was engaged many of them accepted the offer of amnesty from Santa Anna, the Mexican president and general in charge of the siege. Notably, Juan Sequin left under orders from Travis to seek recruits, leading to his pivotal role at San Jacinto. At that battle, amidst cries of "Remember the Alamo," the Tejanos fighting for Sam Houston were instructed to paste white bands on their hats and breastplates to differentiate them from the

Mexicans fighting under Santa Anna. As we've seen, massive was the ensuing slaughter of Mexican soldiers.

While Tejanos were ambivalent and defensive, the Texians were, by contrast, basically optimistic. They were riding the crest of a historical legacy of success. Twice in recent history their forebearers, including some of the Texas pioneers themselves, had twisted the tail of the British lion, first in their revolutionary struggle of 1776 and following, and then in the War of 1812. With these relatively recent victories as a legacy, it was with a feeling of restless abandon that the Anglo-Americans came to Texas. Seeking initially to work within the Mexican sociopolitical network that greeted them upon their arrival, they would eventually burst the cords that bound them to that system. As we have seen, the declaration formalizing the bursting of those cords was forged at Washington-on-the-Brazos.

The successful war for independence from Mexico, leading to a republic in Texas modeled on the U.S. system, lent fodder to what was coming to be perceived as an inevitable movement for Anglo-American dominance of the whole North American continent. With Texas's annexation to the United States in 1845, that movement received a name. When John O'Sullivan coined the term Manifest Destiny, he believed that God had given the United States the mission to spread republican democracy throughout North America.

O'Sullivan's invocation of God and destiny hit a common chord with U.S. citizens, based largely along the lines of Protestant Christian reasoning stretching back to the founding of the country. Two of the key thinkers upon whom the founders of the United States political system relied most heavily in writing the constitution were British intellectuals William Blackstone and John Locke. Blackstone reckoned that God had established a natural law or standard by which to govern the whole world. It was the duty of men to reference that standard in their dealings not only with members of their own culture but with other cultures as well. Through appeal to that standard as a reference point, opined the disciples of Blackstone, political and social systems could find common ground.

John Locke added the idea of God-given "natural rights." This was the view that God had ordained that those who accepted his standard as a reference point should be granted certain rights of privilege. Locke emphasized that rights should belong to the thrifty and rational, not the shiftless and lazy. For Locke, along with natural rights came the duty to act responsibly toward God and man. In 1776, Thomas Jefferson, as the key architect of the U.S. Declaration of Independence, incorporated Locke's concept of natural rights into that pivotal document.

The third source cited as a major influence on the founding fathers of the U.S. system was the Frenchman Joseph de Secondat, the Baron de Montesquieu. Arguing from the biblical premise, Montesquieu reasoned that given the biblical view of the fall from the Garden of Eden, inherent in man's nature was a tendency toward evil. Hence, he called for checks and balances in politics and society. Picking up heavily on this point was the father of the U.S. Constitution, James Madison. Interestingly, Montesquieu, a Catholic, believed that the "Catholic Religion is most agreeable to a Monarchy, and the Protestant to a Republic....A religion which has no visible head is more agreeable to the independence of the climate than that which has [a visible head]."

By the time the early Anglo-American pioneers came to form a majority in Texas, the United States had experienced two phases of what historians describe as a "Great Awakening." This term referred to a revival or rekindling of the views and religious roots of such thinkers as Blackstone, Locke and Montesquieu. Somewhat modifying the effect of the religious revival, the United States had also experienced two waves of an intellectual movement that historians label the Enlightenment.

The Enlightenment stemmed initially from the Italian Renaissance, but it was largely by way of the French Revolution of 1789 that its precepts found root in the United States. Under the influence of French thinkers such as Jean Jacques Rousseau, the French version of the concept centered on the "rights of man." Instead of God's will, Rousseau emphasized the need to focus on the "common will" of a given society as the reference point for political and social communication. As a result, society, rather than God, became the primary reference point. Upon losing touch with the personal Transcendent God as the reference point for morality, the concept of natural rights took on abstract connotations. Rights became consonant with the ever-changing mores of society, thus losing their ties to the absolutes inherent in biblical standards.

The emerging concept of society-conditioned natural rights had a profound impact on intercultural relationships. We will explore the interactions of the Anglo-Texians first with Tejanos, then with the Indians.

ANGLO-SAXONS VS. TEJANOS

As our discussions up to this point imply, an understanding of the cultural clash between Anglo-Texians and Tejanos begins with religion, Protestant vs. Catholic. Texians were nonplused over the insistence of the Mexican government on recognizing only Catholic worship as legitimate, for the Anglo-American heritage was fundamentally Protestant. Here the emphasis was on "Christian living" and the responsibility of the individual. The minister was subordinate to the congregation, and there were competing sects; most prominent in Mexican Texas were the Methodists, Baptists and Presbyterians.

During the era of Mexican Texas, Anglo-Texians contrived various means to finesse the official Mexican policy of allowing the practice only of Catholicism. This meant, for instance, that marriages among Anglo-Texians often began as civil affairs. There would be some type of civil ceremony bonding the couple until the arrival of a priest could make the union official. A problem was that priests were few and far between in Texas.

One way around the problem for the Anglo-Texians was the Sunday school. Technically, a Sunday school meeting was not a church service per se. Pioneering this idea was Thomas J. Pilgrim. We met him in the last chapter, as the proprietor of a school at San Felipe de Austin. Related to his school, Mr. Pilgrim also started a Sunday school at San Felipe in 1829. Most of the education in Anglo-Texian schools in early Texas was Christian-based, much of it taught by ministers.

Huntsville was a center of missionary activity in the early years. In addition to James W. and Daniel Parker, Z.N. Morrell and Moses Speer, mentioned earlier, a female missionary of the Presbyterian denomination, Melinda Rankin, was prominent at the beginning of Texas statehood. In 1847, she came to Texas and taught for a while at the Huntsville Male and Female Academy. All the while, she was writing for religious publications. Then, with Reverend W. Adair, she opened a school off the Trinity River at the then-booming town of Cincinnati. While there, she wrote her first book, *Texas in 1850*. Melinda Rankin's main objective in coming to Texas was to minister to Mexicans. Consequently, she soon left the area of our Cradle Road for adventures in missionary work to Tejanos along the Mexican border. Her work carried her across the border into Mexico itself.

Meanwhile, there were continuing tensions between Tejanos and Anglo-Texians before and during the republic era, based fundamentally in differences of religious perspective. Whereas Protestantism fit well the tendency toward abstract thinking among the Anglo-Texians, Catholicism was a better fit for the person-oriented cultural mindset of the Tejanos. In Tejano culture, heir to the parent culture of New Spain, class dominated. Though there were few of the top-level pure Spanish (the old *peninsulares* who were born in Spain) among the Tejanos, *criollos* (of pure Spanish descent but born in the New World) there were plenty, complete with the traditional *patrón-peón* dichotomy in social relations. So it was, therefore, that the propensities of Spanish Catholicism better suited the temperament of the Tejanos, with the priest-led rather than congregation-led social order.

Anecdotal confirmation of the stratification evident in Tejano society is seen in an incident during the heat of battle during the Texas Revolution. Along with a Tejano cohort named Plácido Benavides, the legendary Jim Bowie, married to a Tejana of aristocratic lineage, badgered a lowly Tejano herdsman in an effort to extract information about a strange matter. In his article entitled "Efficient to the Cause," Stephen Hardin, a scholar of the Tejano psyche, assesses the mindset of the Tejano social structure reflected in this incident:

> *Tejano society consisted of ricos and pobres. Military commandants, government officials, successful financiers, and large ranch owners constituted an influential elite. Providing stark contrast were the mixed-blood peones, common laborers who lived out their lives in drudgery and service to the patrones. Bowie had joined one of the wealthiest and oldest families in Texas; it was only natural that he would have adopted their attitudes towards the lowly pobres. One of the province's leading oligarchs, Plácido Benavides, more properly, Don Plácido, since his position as an alcalde and land owner entitled him to the honorific, would have had few qualms about abusing a herdsman, a creature clearly his social inferior.*

Another significant contrast to the abstractness of Protestantism lay in the greater emphasis of the Tejano religion on ceremony, with a major focus on festivals celebrating the Virgin of Guadalupe and various saint days. Timothy M. Matovina describes the procession accompanying one of these ceremonies in Mexican Texas in his article "Between Two Worlds":

> *An elegantly adorned image of our Lady of Guadalupe was the principal ritual object* [as well as a cross and] *a banner of the church. Priest and the general populace both took part in the procession. Young girls dressed in white and bearing candles…were the immediate attendants of the Guadalupian image.…Fiddlers also participated.…Sixty members of the militia served as escorts. The rosary was prayed and…religious hymns honoring the mother of God were sung.…Guns* [were] *being fired as part of the devotion, and cannons and bells* [were] *sounding as well.*

The attitudinal conditioning via religion for the personal touch over the abstract carried over into a contrast in political style between the Anglo-Texian and the Tejanos. For the Tejanos, politics, reflecting their religion, also was more personal. Tejano tendencies veered toward a focus on petitioning higher political authority for relief. This was in contrast to the more raucous tendency of the Anglo-Texians, oriented toward demanding their natural rights to take matters into their own hands and form a completely new government, as in 1836. The various consultations and other meetings leading up to Texas independence from Mexico were predominantly attended by Anglo-Texians, with few Tejanos invited or interested in attending. For example, only two Tejanos were signers of the Texas Declaration of Independence at Old Washington.

Although Mexico had adopted a liberal constitution in 1824, its effects were transient. Within ten years, Mexico found itself under the rule of the dictator Santa Anna, prompting the Texians to engage in their act of rebellion. By 1835, Austin realized that he had been rather naive to expect a radical change in the perception of a people just because they had a liberal constitution. By the time the Anglo-Texians entered the showdown with Santa Anna, Austin not only had realized his naivete in relation to the generating of a political culture conducive to U.S.-style democracy in an alien land, but he also began, for the first time, to openly advocate freedom of religion. Specifically, he called explicitly for a revival of the dominant Protestantism of his U.S. heritage as a means to foster cultural conditioning for U.S.-style democracy.

In a letter to Mrs. Holley, dated January 7, 1836, Austin made explicit the connection of the Texas Revolution to the religious tradition of the United States:

Large contributions have been made in the United States for the extension of Christianity over the South Sea Islands by means of Missionary societies. Is not our cause quite as important and sacred? We are trying to banish from our homes religious intolerance and despotism and to establish in the place of it liberty and freedom of conscience. How many thousands of pious families of all denominations might find a home and become the proprietors of the soil of Texas—the best soil and climate accessible to North Americans—if religious tolerance were once firmly rooted there! Religion, morality, the arts and sciences, the great sources of liberty—which is in fact, the cause of mankind—all unite in calling upon the free, the generous, the enterprising and the pious, to step forward in aid of Texas. We expect aid from the religious portion of the community, and the pulpit will pour out its eloquent voice to the people in the cause of all free churches— the cause of truth and justice.

Austin's belated perception of the cultural distance between the precepts of Mexican culture and those of Anglo-American-style republican democracy echoed words written earlier by Thomas Jefferson. At the time of Mexican independence from Spain, Jefferson had written the following words:

I wish I could give better hopes for our southern brethren. The achievement of their independence is no longer a question, but it is a very serious one. What will become of them? Ignorance and bigotry like other insanities, are incapable of self-government. They will fall under military despotisms, and become the murderous tools of the ambitions of their respective Bonaparte.

Even as contrasting religious and philosophical underpinnings were widening the cultural gap between the Tejanos and Anglo-Texians, two Mexican military invasions in 1842 enhanced cultural dissension between them. One repercussion of this growing cultural dissension appeared in the Texas Constitutional Convention of 1845, as evidenced in a proposal that suffrage be extended exclusively to the "free white populace."

Tejano voting rights, however, were preserved in the new state of Texas. This was due largely to a resolute Tejano taking matters into his own hands, challenging the Texian establishment. Addressing the assemblage at the convention, José Antonio Navarro contended, with success, that inclusion of the "white" in electoral legislation was "odious" and "ridiculous."

ANGLO-TEXIANS VS. THE INDIANS

One problem some Anglo-Texians had with Tejanos lay in the prevalence among the latter of *mestizos*, people of mixed Spanish and Indian heritage. The Anglo-Texians' problem with the Indian part of that mixture was in part philosophical. The cyclical thinking of the Indian placed him in tune with nature and the reckoning of time and the seasons. He felt at one with "brother" bear, coyote and so forth and with the rhythms of the earth. On the other hand, as heir of the Enlightenment, the abstractness of the Anglo-Texian coupled with his pragmatic lifestyle conditioned in him a mindset bent on conquering instead of revering nature. Nature became thus objectified, an object to be addressed and mastered. Viewed as an obstacle to his conquest of nature, the Indian also became, for the Anglo-Texan, an object to be mastered.

There were, however, those—such as Stephen Austin and Sam Houston—who sought to bring the Indian into a trading system attuned to that of the white man. Toward this end, Austin suggested three alternatives. One was the incorporation of a company to assume overall responsibility for the Indian trade in Texas. This company would operate from a base of set laws. His second alternative centered on the establishment of factories for the production of supplies for the Indians. Finally, the third alternative lay in granting licenses to individual traders. Austin endorsed the first alternative, a formal company.

Austin, though, was realistic, maintaining that along with trade, the Anglo-Texans should form militias. This he did for his colony, building on support not only from Anglo-Texans but also from friendly Indians in his area, such as the Bidai and Coushatta.

Other colonists in Austin's area were likewise skillful negotiators with local Indians. For instance, Jesse Grimes habitually attended meetings with local Bidai and the Coushatta and Kickapoo when they encamped near his home. There was one particular Bidai warrior who, on occasions when Mr. Grimes was away from home for an extended period, would watch over his family.

Another significant figure in the area was Jacob Shannon. Jacob ran unsuccessfully for the position of sheriff in the government of Washington Municipality. Jacob operated a trading post near the present town of Dobbin. A friend of his was an important personage among the Bidai. That Bidai once told Jacob, "You know that dreams come true." Jacob responded in the affirmative. The Bidai then stated that in his dream, Jacob had given him a suit of clothes and a fine saddle. Not wanting to alienate the Bidai, Jacob obliged him. However, Jacob later told him that, he, Jacob, also had a dream, in which the Bidai had given him a choice section of land. The Bidai reportedly obliged Jacob, but with the statement that neither should dream again about such things.

There were, though, some problems between the colonists and renegade Indians. We have mentioned, for example, the tragic story of Mrs. Taylor near Roans Prairie. In regard to containing the threat of Indians coming from north of the Cradle Road area, we have mentioned, for example, J.G.W. Pierson and his Montgomery brothers-in-law and their key roles in Robertson's Colony.

In her book *Frontier Blood*, Jo Ella Powell Exley isolates the sentiments of the early Anglo-Texians about the Indians in their midst:

> *There were two very different kinds of Indians in Texas: Caddos, half civilized from Louisiana, mixed with remnants of other tribes from farther east, and the wild Indians, also immigrants but of much earlier date than the Caddos. Among the wild Indians the Comanches were the most powerful, they claimed the sovereignty of Texas. They regarded the whites on the Colorado and west of it as a different race from those on the Brazos and in the east generally. In fact, they regarded the whites, like themselves, as divided into tribes, and so made war on the western whites while they considered the eastern ones their friends. The Caddos were much better informed, and knowing the difficulties that might arise from the wild Indian depredations, they did not themselves go to the Colorado River. But the people of the Colorado believed that Caddos harbored their enemies and traded with them for stolen horses, in their vexation they even accused the Brazos whites of such conduct.*

Among the Anglo-Texans, Sam Houston was very much on the wavelength of the Indians, being an adopted member of the Cherokee. Like Austin, he sought diligently to reach accommodation with them on several levels. On the other hand, Sam Houston's successor as president of the Republic of Texas, Mirabeau Lamar, took the concept of objectification alluded to above to the logical conclusion, driving many of the east Texas tribes, most notably the Cherokee, out of Texas through military force.

By 1854, the Texas government had allotted land for two Indian reservations off the North Brazos River. There the government sought to instill in the Indian the white man's ways of looking at the world and of making a living. By 1858, various problems—such as lack of good land, encroaching whites and other problems—led the government to send all but the Alabama-Coushatta tribes off to Indian Territory in what later became the state of Oklahoma. It would be another twenty years before all the Comanche, Apache and Tonkawas were reconciled to reservations.

Also affecting our Cradle Road area was the issue of slavery. It is to a discussion of that pivotal issue as it affected our area of study that we now turn.

CHAPTER 13

THE LEGACY OF MANIFEST DESTINY №3

THE ISSUE OF RACE

When John O'Sullivan coined the term Manifest Destiny in 1845, he was thinking of the special destiny of the Anglo-Saxon race to enter new territory and set up a republican government. However, O'Sullivan touched roots that predated the Texas Revolution, running deep in United States history. As far back as Puritan America, John Winthrop wrote his famous "City on a Hill" sermon in 1630. Here he called for the establishment of a virtuous community that would serve as a shining example to the Old World.

Similarly, in 1776 Thomas Paine wrote his influential pamphlet *Common Sense*, with the message that the United States revolution would create a new and better society. "We have it in our power," he wrote, "to begin the world over again. A situation similar to the present has not happened since the days of Noah until now. The birthday of a new world is at hand."

Following the theme of Thomas Paine and John Winthrop, United States secretary of state John Quincy Adams wrote the following:

> *The whole continent of North America appears to be destined and kept by Divine Providence to be peopled by one nation, speaking one language, professing one general system of religion and political principles, and accustomed to one general tenor of social usage and customs. For the common happiness of them all, for their peace and prosperity, I believe it is indispensable that they should be associated in one Federal Union.*

Manifest Destiny was key to John Quincy Adams's foreign policy as secretary of state under President James Monroe. As architect of Monroe's famous doctrine of 1823, Adams deemed it the destiny of the United States to oversee the development of Latin America to keep the area free from further contamination at the hands of the Old World of European dynasties.

Paradox of Manifest Destiny

The perspective of the United States as the model and enforcer of the culture of the New World would meet a paradox when the United States went to war with Mexico from 1846 until 1848. Mexico had never recognized Texas's independence; therefore, when the United States annexed Texas in 1845, war was inevitable. During that war, there were cries from many quarters for the United States to annex all of Mexico. The paradox lay in the view on the one hand that it would be good for the United States to take over Mexico, while on the other hand there were those who believed such an act would be bad for the United States.

Among those expressing concern was Ulysses S. Grant, who was a participant in that war and destined to play a major role as commanding general of the northern forces in an even more devasting conflict later. After that later war, the Civil War, Grant opined as follows:

> *The Southern rebellion was largely the outgrowth of the Mexican War. Nations, like individuals, are punished for their transgressions. We got our punishment in the most sanguinary and expensive war of modern times.*

Grant was correct. The Mexican War played a key role in framing issues, setting the stage for a major conflict between American states. One link lay in the Wilmot Proviso. Introduced into the U.S. House of Representatives under the auspices of Congressman David Wilmot, representative from Pennsylvania, this rider to an appropriation bill of 1846 related to the Mexican War stated:

> *Provided, That, as an express and fundamental condition to the acquisition of any territory from the Republic of Mexico by the United States, by virtue of any treaty which may be negotiated between them, and to the use by the Executive of the moneys herein appropriated, neither slavery nor*

involuntary servitude shall ever exist in any part of said territory, except for
crime, whereof the party which shall first be duly convicted.

Though the Wilmot Proviso failed to pass in the Congress, its precepts set the stage for the key political issue of the country for the next fifteen or so years, that of slavery. Though the proviso brought the issue into the open, slavery failed to generate a major conflagration in the nation until 1861, due largely to the Compromise of 1850, an omnibus bill linking five core issues facing the country, each related to slavery.

Three of these core issues related directly to the Mexican cession after the Mexican-American War. One of these concerned the boundaries of Texas, a slave state. While its southern border would now stretch beyond the Nueces to the Rio Grande, in exchange for $10 million with which to pay off its debts, Texas surrendered claims to territory in present New Mexico, Oklahoma, Colorado, Kansas and Wyoming. The second issue concerned California, which had been ceded to the United States as a result of the war. California would enter the United States as a free state. Third, New Mexico Territory—which included much of present Arizona and other states also coming under U.S. sovereignty after the Mexican War—would enter the Union according to the wishes of the people at the time.

The fourth and fifth components of the Compromise of 1850 held a more direct relation to the issue of slavery. One of these focused on the nation's capital, Washington, D.C. In the District of Columbia, the slave trade would cease, although not the institution of slavery itself.

It was the fifth component of the Compromise of 1850 that generated the most immediate heat. This was the Fugitive Slave Law. Among its tenets were the following. Any federal marshal or other official who did not arrest an alleged runaway slave would be liable for a fine of $1,000. The official was obliged to act even on an unsupported sworn testimony of ownership. This was controversial because the suspected slave could not ask for a jury trial or even testify on his or her own behalf. Any person aiding a suspected runaway slave—by, for example, offering food or lodging—would be subjected to a $1,000 fine and a six-month stint of imprisonment. Among the repercussions of the Fugitive Slave Law was the galvanizing of a readership primed to be influenced strongly on reading Harriet Beecher Stowe's classic novel *Uncle Tom's Cabin*, depicting the ills of slavery.

The Compromise of 1850 bought time for the nation to pursue conciliation, but other events, most notably the Kansas-Nebraska Act of 1854, neutralized many of the positive effects. That act essentially nullified the Missouri Compromise of 1820, which had prohibited slavery north of the 36°30′ parallel. It allowed Kansas and Nebraska, both north of the 40th parallel, the right to decide the issue of slavery in their respective impending states via popular sovereignty.

Other issues than slavery were indeed instrumental in leading to the Civil War, such as a controversial tariff. None, however, like slavery, touched the chords of culture so vital to the harmony of a nation. We turn now to an analysis of the phenomenon of slavery in Texas during the pre-republic and the republic eras, followed by a comparative study of same in the post-republic era of the Cradle of Texas Road.

SLAVERY IN MEXICAN TEXAS, 1821–36

Mexicans generally abhorred slavery. However, the government allowed it in Texas, under certain parameters, due largely to the influence of the Tejano elite. That elite stood to gain from conditions surrounding an influx of a market in cotton. Although slavery itself was thus quasi-legal, both national and state laws banned the actual trade in slaves. The result was that Anglo-Americans could bring their family slaves to Texas with them, but once here, they were limited as to the trade in slaves across the border with Texas.

In Stephen Austin's initial, but aborted, contract for his original colony, a head of household was to receive 640 acres. Had he a wife, an additional 320 acres would be added, and with each child still another 100 acres would swell his holdings. Given the Mexican qualms about slavery, it is interesting that each slave that the Anglo-Texians brought would yield yet another 80 acres.

Though they could not engage in the slave trade across the national border, the Anglo-Texians could buy and sell slaves within the state until the year 1840. The grandchildren of these slaves were slated to be freed gradually at a certain age. When the Mexican government inferred in 1827 that it might emancipate slaves before the promised 1840 deadline, some Anglo-Texians took this as their cue to have their illiterate slaves sign indenture contracts. These typically bound slaves for ninety-nine years to work off their purchase price, upkeep and transportation to Texas.

Seeing through this facade of justice, many Mexicans perceived this as similar to the debt peonage inflicted upon their lower class historically at the hands of their former Spanish masters. Partly as a result, in September of 1829, in commemoration of Mexico's independence from those

Spanish masters, Mexican president Vicente Ramón Guerrero issued an order of emancipation of all slaves. Again, however, through the influence of important Tejanos, Stephen Austin's colonists received an exemption from this order.

SLAVERY IN THE REPUBLIC OF TEXAS, 1836–45

The Texas Constitution of 1836 addressed four aspects of the slave trade. First and fundamentally, it legalized slavery. Then it formulated two key provisions of prohibition against the Texas congress. One of these prohibited congress from restricting the importation of slaves from the United States. The other prohibited congress from emancipating the slaves. The fourth point established slave codes, defining the status of slaves in Texas society.

Given these four rather harsh items, a section of the book *Adventure in Glory*, under the authorship of Seymour V. Connor, PhD, is significant to our narrative. The reference is to the first session of the Texas congress at its new base in Houston in 1837:

> *There were a number of free Negroes in Texas at the time of the* [Texas] *Declaration of Independence, many of whom had fought valorously in the Revolution....It is noteworthy that this session of Congress, in an "Act for the Relief of Free Persons of Color," tried within the framework of the members' own prejudices to render justice to these people. The Free Negro never attained the status of citizen, but he received land grants (and was assessed taxes) and was in the main treated more fairly in Texas than he would have been in almost any state in the United States at the time.*

Now we will address some comparative numbers and percentages of slaves in our Cradle of Texas Road area between the republic and Civil War eras. We will center on the three counties that emerged completely within that area: Grimes, Walker and Montgomery Counties.

GRIMES COUNTY

In 1850, Grimes County had 1,680 slaves plus 2 free African Americans. Whites accounted for 2,326 persons for a total population of 4,006. Slaves, then, were 41 percent of the population in 1850. By 1855, the county tax rolls revealed 3,124 slaves, or an 86 percent increase over the 1850 level.

According to the 1860 census, the number of slaves had by then increased to 5,468. This was a 75 percent increase over 1855 and 225 percent more than 1850. There was by 1860 a total population of 10,320, with 4,852 of them white. Slaves, then, constituted 53 percent of the population in 1860. This means that while the white population doubled between 1850 and 1860, the slave population tripled.

In 1860, Grimes County had 505 slaveholders. Of these, 77 were classified as planters, meaning they held 20 or more slaves. In 1859, just two years previously, there were 42 planters in the county. So, in the two years from 1858 to 1860, the number of planters in Grimes County increased by 83.3 percent. Furthermore, Grimes County was one of only seventeen counties in the state in which the average number of slaves per slaveholder was greater than 10.

WALKER COUNTY

In 1850, slaves numbered 1,301, and there were recorded no free African Americans. Whites accounted for 2,663 for a total population of 3,964. Slaves, then, were 32.8 percent of the total population in 1850.

Between 1850 and 1860, slaves increased to 4,135. This was a 217.8 percent increase in 1860 over the number in 1850. By 1860, there was a total population or 8,191, with 4,056 of them white. Slaves, then, were 50.4 percent of the population. This meant that while the white population had less than doubled, the Black population had more than tripled over ten years.

By 1860, 58 percent of white families owned slaves: 376 of 646. Approximately 80 percent of these owned fewer than 20 slaves. This would leave some 75 planters in Walker County in 1860.

MONTGOMERY COUNTY

In 1850, slaves numbered 945 out of a total population of 2,384 while whites accounted for 1,439 persons. Slaves, then, were about 40 percent of the population. By 1860, the total population was 5,479, with whites accounting for 3,063 to 2,416 slaves. So, slaves accounted for 44 percent. While whites, then, had increased by 112.8 percent, slaves had increased by 155.6 percent, or more than doubled.

CONCLUSIONS FOR GRIMES, WALKER AND MONTGOMERY COUNTIES

From 1850 to 60, the greatest increase in the slave population was in Grimes County, 225 percent. Second was Walker County with an increase of 217.8 percent and third was Montgomery County with an increase of 155.6 percent.

In 1860, the total number of slaves and slave percentages of the total population were as follows: For Grimes County, there were 5,468 slaves, or 53 percent of the population. In Walker County, the total number was 4,135 slaves, for 50.4 percent of the population, and for Montgomery County, there were 2,416 slaves, or 44 percent of the population.

ASSESSMENT OF MANIFEST DESTINY IN EARLY TEXAS

Our study to this point has demonstrated the Anglo-American spirit behind Manifest Destiny. It has also shown the penchant for compromise, up to a point, in relations with Tejanos and Indians. Though African American slavery was seen to be prevalent and forceful, there were elements in play to address slavery's brutal realities.

THE DESTINY OF MANIFEST DESTINY

Though marred by slavery, the Republic and State of Texas were heir to a tradition imbued, though imperfectly, with the goals and ideals of equality.

The theme of Manifest Destiny took root in a ship called *Arabella* in 1630, through an oration from the governor of Massachusetts Bay Colony, John Winthrop. Most poignant was his line about forging a "city on a hill" as a beacon of light to the world. The address invoked the blessings of God on the grand project that was America. The call to Christianity again echoed grandly with the Second Great Awakening in the 1740s, as ministers like Jonathan Edwards and Charles Finney called for a return to those religious roots of destiny.

It was within the echoes of that great awakening that Thomas Jefferson wrote the immortal words of our Declaration of Independence, featuring the lines "We hold these truths to be self-evident, that all men are created equal and endowed by their Creator with certain unalienable rights." Jefferson then marked the path to that government: "To secure these rights, governments are instituted among men, securing their just powers from the consent of the governed." The context here was a society of the governed attuned to the theme of the declaration. Accordingly, Jefferson and numerous others, including Sam Houston, called for a society characterized by "intelligence and virtue."

As indicated in our prelude to this book, in line with this clarion call were the words of John O'Sullivan in 1839, stating that the United States was a country without a past, only a future centered on its religious tradition. Six years later, in 1845, he identified that tradition with Texas, as Texas emerged from a republic as a state of the United States. Thus inspired, O'Sullivan labeled that tradition "Manifest Destiny." Just nine years previously, in 1836, the Texas Declaration of Independence from Mexico had referenced identity with the U.S. Constitution. At the same time, a letter from Stephen F. Austin to Andrew Jackson explicitly identified the Texas "generation of 1836" with that of the United States in 1776.

Now hear Lincoln's words from his Gettysburg Address, also linked to the generation of 1776.

> *Four score and seven years ago, our fathers set forth upon this continent a new nation dedicated to the proposition that all men are created equal. Now we are engaged in a great civil war, testing whether that nation, or any nation so conceived and so dedicated can long endure.*

Lincoln then expressed the purpose before the nation, to "take increased devotion to that cause for which they gave the last full measure of devotion."

In step with Lincoln's thinking was the "Liberator of Texas" and the first president of the Republic of Texas, Sam Houston. Reflections of this thesis are found in our following and final chapter, on Sam Houston and his fabulous slave, Joshua Houston.

CHAPTER 14

SAM HOUSTON AND HIS HEIR, THE FABULOUS JOSHUA

he pivotal figure of our Cradle of Texas Road is Sam Houston. Let's explore Houston's relationship with his phenomenal slave and namesake, Joshua Houston.

INTRODUCTION

When Sam Houston married Margaret Lea of Alabama in 1840, his life changed. The Christianity that had been there all along, but reticent, waxed full blown, leading eventually to formal baptism. Along the way, his impact on his favorite slave, Joshua, a holdover of Margaret's from Alabama, was immeasurable. Joshua became the caretaker of Sam and Margaret's growing family when Sam was out of town, and he traveled with Sam Houston on numerous trips, witnessing firsthand the great man in action. Along the way, thanks to the at the time illegal leniency of Sam and Margaret, Joshua learned to read and do basic arithmetic. Within the Christian context, Joshua Houston became a model of education linked to virtue.

Evidence of Joshua's intrepid character is found in a reference from the book about Joshua *From Slave to Statesman* by Patricia Smith Prather and Jane Clements Monday. The setting was the time immediately after the death of Sam Houston in Huntsville, Texas, in 1863. Margaret was

Left: This seventy-seven-foot monument to Sam Houston, just south of Huntsville off Interstate 45, attests to the great esteem Texans feel for this remarkable man. *Courtesy of Booking.com.*

Right: Joshua Houston, slave of the Sam Houston family, amazing both as a slave and later as a freed man. *Courtesy of BlackPast.org.*

in the community of Independence. Joshua had braved the volatile Civil War atmosphere to ride, alone, the near seventy miles from Huntsville to Independence to visit Margaret. In his saddlebags were his life savings. Prather and Monday relay then the following:

> *Uncle Joshua waited until Mrs. Houston finished her dinner to ask her if he could talk to her alone....* [He] *laid an old leather bag on the table...* [and] *told her there was over $2000 in gold and United States currency in the bag and that he wanted her to use every cent of it....* [She] *was so overcome with the unselfish devotion which one of her slaves had shown, that she could not talk for a minute. But she handed the money back to Uncle Joshua and said "It is noble of you to want to help us. You have no idea how I appreciate your kindness, and I shall never forget it, but I cannot accept your savings....I want you to take your money and do just what I know General Houston would want you to do with it, if he were here and that is to give your own boys and girls a good education."*

The same source linked Joshua's son, Samuel W. Houston, to his legacy:

> *Joshua's four sons and four daughters continued his educational legacy,
> each in his or her own way, but Samuel W. chose perhaps the most
> traditional road. Samuel W. Houston—following the lead of his father
> and of his namesake General Sam Houston—seemed destined to become
> an educational leader. He possessed the drive to establish a school which
> would become known as the "Tuskegee of Texas" and which would train
> yet another generation of scholars to build on the educational legacy that
> began long before he was born.*

JOSHUA AND SAM HOUSTON

Born in 1822, Joshua spent his early years on the plantation of Temple Lea
in Marion, Alabama. On the elder Lea's death in 1834, Joshua became the
property of Temple's daughter, Margaret Lea. By that time, Joshua had
already become well exposed to the gospel of Christ. Temple had been a
lay minister and he and his wife, Nancy, often included their slaves in Bible
study and services. As Margaret and Sam would continue later, the Leas'
slaves received the opportunity to learn to read via studying scripture. This,
then, was a major advantage that Joshua received in comparison to most of
the slaves of the old South: he had masters who practiced Christian charity
in allowing their slaves to learn to read.

SAM AND MARGARET MARRY: EARLY TIME IN TEXAS

It was in 1839 that Sam Houston passed through Marion, en route to visit
Andrew Jackson. It was during this time that he met the fair Margaret and was
immediately infatuated by her. Her parents were understandably cautious in
the face of the vast twenty-six-year age difference between them, Margaret
being at the time twenty years old. After a rigorous time of courtship and
toeing the line in obedience to Nancy, Nancy relented. Margaret and Sam
became husband and wife. Then it was off to Texas for the entourage, which
included Margaret's favorite slaves, Joshua and Eliza.

In Texas, the family moved from place to place, the key site being Cedar
Point near Galveston. Other sites were Houston, Austin, Washington-on-
the-Brazos, Huntsville (three different sites) and Independence.

Undoubtedly the most exotic home of Sam Houston was the Steamboat House, shown here in Huntsville, now in Sam Houston Park across from Sam Houston State University. *Courtesy of Sam Houston Memorial Museum Complex.*

JOSHUA MEETS WILLIAM GOYENS

Meanwhile, Sam Houston was traveling. At one of the major stops, Nacogdoches, Joshua was with him and met an enterprising African American, a free man, William Goyens, who much impressed him. Goyens was a pillar of the city, a blacksmith, manufacturer of wagons and the owner of thousands of acres of land. Furthermore, he spoke the dialect of the local Indians, thus helping Sam Houston immensely in his dealings with them. From his relationship with William Goyens, Joshua could see, firsthand, the potential of the African American, once receiving the opportunity to excel.

Sam Houston had visited Marion and met Margaret just after his first term as president of the Republic of Texas. Joshua was with the general through his later term as congressman, then again when he was president of the republic. During the era that Texas was assuming the position of a state of the Union, Andrew Jackson lay dying in Tennessee. Along with Sam and Margaret, Joshua made that fateful journey to the Jackson home, the Hermitage outside of Nashville, to arrive just an hour late; the former general turned president had just died.

RAVEN HILL HOME

Upon returning to settle briefly at Raven Hill outside of Huntsville, Sam received the vote to become one of Texas's first two senators to represent the state in Washington, D.C. That year of 1846 was significant for various reasons, one being the impending war with Mexico, which country had never reconciled itself to Texas's independence; now that it was a state of the United States, war clouds loomed. Interestingly, in pursuit of that war, at Fanthorp Inn in Anderson stayed temporarily several individuals who would loom large in United States history. It is believed that among them were Ulysses Grant, Robert E. Lee and Jefferson Davis.

Also, in 1846, Walker County received birth with Huntsville its county seat. The county had broken off from Montgomery County in that year. At the time, Huntsville consisted of three stores—Smithers, Gibbs and McDonald—a stagecoach rendezvous known as the Globe Tavern and a mercantile store under the proprietorship of Pleasant Gray. Gray had founded the town in 1835, naming it for his hometown in Alabama.

It was to Huntsville that Joshua would drive Margaret on Sundays the fourteen miles to attend church. Reverend Frances Creath was pastor of the Huntsville Baptist Church, which held services in the Brick Academy, an educational site erected a few years earlier.

While he was becoming known to the key personages of the town and region, Joshua was also developing proficiency as a blacksmith, wagon master and even as a veterinarian. Additionally, given his knowledge of math and reading, he was trusted to make family purchases downtown and, for security, his freedoms extended to the right to carry firearms. As already indicated, he was, was there a lull in his duties, given the freedom to work on his own and keep most, if not all, of his earnings.

Of educational import to Joshua were his visits accompanying Sam Houston some fourteen miles from Raven Hill to the abode of Sam's brother-in-law, Vernon Lea. Here, at Council Hill, was one of the main sites at which Sam visited with his old friends, the Indians. This was significant, as it appears that the slaves of Temple Lea in Alabama had been kept separated from Indians as much as possible.

Jumping the Broom with Anneliza

Another freedom of Joshua's, up to a point, was the freedom to have a mate. Joshua's lived at another plantation; her name was Anneliza. With her, he had several children, whom he attended as best he could. According to the tradition of the times, children of such a union were considered the property of the master of the female. While formal marriages were forbidden to slaves, an unofficial ceremony sealed the union in the minds of their cohorts. It consisted of "jumping the broom." The female would first jump over a broom held at a diagonal angle for the purpose, to be followed by the male. Then, in tandem, they would jump to the place of beginning.

Evidence of Sam Houston's rejuvenated Christian faith lies in his practice of holding gospel gatherings after entertaining guests at a meal at the Houston home. The guests would assemble on the porch, in chairs that Joshua probably helped arrange, to hear Sam Houston himself read a body of scripture then proffer an exegesis. At that point, family and guests sang hymns, then the session ended with a prayer.

The Woodlands Home

When the Houston family moved to the outskirts of Huntsville to their home called "The Woodlands," their guests would often include Indians. Indians were known to drop by and camp on the grounds of the Houston farm when they were traveling through.

One of Sam Houston's guests, who would, like Houston, play a primary role in Joshua's growing perception of the importance of education, was Colonel George Grant. Among other enterprises, Colonel Grant operated a stage line at which Joshua worked on occasion, helping with blacksmithing and other duties.

In the summer of 1851, over the several stage lines running through Huntsville came a large crowd intent on witnessing the dedication of Austin College. Highly impressive to Joshua must have been the scene of Sam Houston holding an umbrella over the college president, Samuel McKinney, while he gave his keynote speech, to shield him from the sun. All around him, Joshua had to have pondered, sprouts of education were blooming. Would he and his progeny ever be able to take advantage of them?

During this era, an excerpt from a letter of Margaret to Sam Houston reveals the daily routine around her home. "We do not keep the children long to their books but allow them an abundance of time for exercise," she wrote, then added: "Thus, one duty after another is taken in regular succession and all confusion is avoided. We have supper before dark that the children may be present at worship."

The young children were privy to these lessons, and all the servants found inclusion in the evening prayer sessions.

When Sam was at home in the Woodlands, he would spend much time at his little office building. There, perhaps his most consistent visitor was Henderson Yoakum, a former mayor in the important town of Murfreesboro, Tennessee, who wrote the first major treatise on Texas history—with quality input from his friend, Sam Houston.

MOVE TO INDEPENDENCE; SAM BAPTIZED

With Sam Houston in Washington, D.C., much of his time as a senator, he saw the utility of moving his family to Independence. Here his children could have access to what was at the time the center of Texas higher education, Baylor College. Also, Margaret's mother and sister were living in Independence.

Joshua witnessed Sam Houston making a gift of $330 to Baylor, to be spent on the education of young ministers. Meanwhile, Margaret was becoming friends with Georgia Burleson, wife of Rufus Burleson, the head of the college at the time. It was on a bright day in 1854 that Reverend Burleson baptized Sam Houston at a spot on Rocky Creek, just below Independence. Margaret was ecstatic. Joshua was impressed. Well known is the comment that Houston allegedly made as Burleson told him his sins were washed away: "I'm sorry for the fish downstream," Sam Houston purportedly uttered.

Founded in 1835 in what is now northern Washington County by J.G.W. Pierson, Robert Stevenson, Colbert Baker and Amasa Burchard, Independence was known at the time as "The Athens of Texas." It was with good reason that the community received such high acclaim for its academic excellence. Here meager beginnings by struggling pioneers laid the foundational roots of both Baylor and Mary Hardin–Baylor Universities.

In the then-wealthiest community in Texas, Baylor University began in 1846 as a coeducational school with twenty-four pupils. In 1851, the school divided into male and female departments. By 1885, however, Independence had declined; the female branch moved to Belton as Mary Hardin–Baylor, and the male branch moved to Waco, carrying the name of Baylor University. Like many other communities of Texas, failure to accept the railroad was a major item in the decline of the community and hence of the college atmosphere.

Buying of Jeff Hamilton

Before Sam Houston left Huntsville for Independence, he noticed a sale going on in front of Gibbs's store. It was the sale of a very young African American boy, who appeared extremely frightened. Observing the situation, Sam discerned that the boy was not well cared for and proceeded on the spot to buy him for $450. He then requested Tom Gibbs, the proprietor of the store, to draw up a bill of sale to the seller, named McKell. He added that he would send Joshua to procure the boy later. From the beginning, the young lad, named Jeff Hamilton, would refer to Joshua as Uncle Josh, while joining other household slaves, such as Eliza Revel, and becoming a lifelong champion of the Houston family.

Jeff must have been amazed the day Sam Houston became alarmed when he saw his slaves eating with their hands. Houston immediately set out for Gibbs's store to purchase cutlery, to return with a good lecture to his slaves on learning some manners. This lesson, too, Joshua would learn: the importance to the establishment of self-discipline and etiquette.

Sam Houston Day in Montgomery

One indication that Sam Houston had empathy and love for people of all races, ages and genders is shown in the reception he received at a special July Fourth celebration in Montgomery, Texas, off the stage route from Houston to Huntsville.

On July 4, 1968, the *Huntsville Item* ran an extended piece by Mrs. Clarence Grogan of Conroe, based on selections from the Hart Addison collection of that town. The article was a treasure chest of observations and reminiscences of that July day in 1857 when it was "Sam Houston Day in Montgomery."

The genesis of the celebration lay in Sam Houston's stopover in Montgomery on his first run for the governorship of Texas. The newspaper article included observations on Sam Houston's character drawn from the assembled at the event, specifically on his ability to relate to all segments of the population. "He loved mankind and made each person feel important as a human being," the article stated, "be they man, woman, child free or slave."

Specifically, the observers portrayed Sam Houston as "one hundred percent masculine." Men "were baffled because they could not anticipate his thinking or his actions. They could feel the x-ray gaze of his going right through them. They knew that he could command and would follow through."

Women, likewise, found Sam Houston extraordinary, as they were "fascinated by his handsome physique and his deep resonant voice…he made them feel that they were loved." The article records that "he adored women from eight to eighty" and that among his writings were the following words: "A woman's influence often controls the destiny of nations" and "Woman's love is the great lover which rouses men to action."

Not only men and women but also children related to and loved Sam Houston, as Houston's great friend Nat H. Davis, among others, made clear. At the Sam Houston Day celebration, Houston was said to have played with the children, giving them mock orders as their commander in chief at San Jacinto.

The article further described Houston's crossing the racial divide. For instance, it remarked on his usual attire of a necklace and an Indian shawl, reminiscent of his youth as an adopted son of Cherokee chief John Jolly. Numerous references centered on his close relationship with Stith, the slave of Dr. James Price, who worked at the Price Hotel.

Even as the people of Montgomery felt drawn to Sam Houston, he was, in turn, drawn to them. "Houston loved the town and people of Montgomery," the piece stated. It quoted Sam as saying, "Montgomery has a heart for Texas."

Unfortunately, the heart of the Texas voting republic was less drawn to Houston in his first try for governor. His great friend Jesse Grimes ran on his ticket for lieutenant governor, and the duo lost that election. The reason lay in their opinions on the slavery issue. Sam, for instance, was the only southerner to vote against the dreaded Kansas-Nebraska Act, which sparked, true to Sam's prediction, much bloodshed and division, as it allowed people to vote their conscience on the question of slavery in the new states.

Back to Huntsville, Independence and On to Austin

Shortly after returning to Huntsville after the latest sojourn in Independence, two of Margaret's servants, Mary and Eliza, joined the Baptist church that they had been attending, sitting upstairs. They received baptism in a pool dug in the Woodlands home yard.

After another move to Independence, a loss in the 1857 race for governor and a win in 1859, Sam Houston moved with his family to Austin. At a rest stop along the way, General Sam asked Jeff Hamilton to recite his ABCs, spell some words and read from a newspaper. Satisfied with Jeff's progress, Sam declared, "Jeff, you will be a learned man yet."

As the presidential race of 1860 heated up, former soldiers from the Battle of San Jacinto assumed the honorary title of vice president to nominate Houston for president on the "people's ticket." One of those vice presidents was Andrew Montgomery. The next year, however, Houston dropped out of the race, claiming that with four opposition candidates splitting the vote, Abraham Lincoln and the Republicans were sure to win, and win they did.

Final Return to Huntsville

Considering Sam Houston's by-then well-known views on the folly of the impending Civil War and the need to preserve the Union, Lincoln offered Union troops to Texas to prevent secession. Houston, however, refused the offer. He furthermore turned down an offer of support from fellow Texans to secure control of the Texas government. Instead, he resigned rather than pay allegiance to the Confederacy, returning to temporary disgrace in Huntsville.

On September 23, 1862, word came of Lincoln's Emancipation Proclamation declaring the end of slavery, which would become the norm in the South in January 1863. The Confederacy had previously declared freeing the slaves to be an illegal act. Sam Houston, however, freed his slaves before the year 1863. Not only that, but on predicting with remarkable accuracy the carnage and results of the Civil War, he began pushing an exotic vision, hoping it would be the diversion to free his countrymen from engaging in that war.

SAM HOUSTON'S VISION
OF A MEXICAN PROTECTORATE

In 1858, Texas was awash in unrest. Talk of civil war abounded, while Indian wars in North Texas along the Red River mirrored Mexican Civil War–induced conflict along the Rio Grande in the south. In September of that volatile year, Sam Houston, by then a lame duck U.S. senator, was again making a pitch for the governor's chair of his beloved Texas. The site was the then-thriving town of Danville, between Conroe and Huntsville. Here Houston wove into a campaign speech the most audacious venture his fertile imagination ever conceived.

The venture entailed nothing less than the United States inflicting upon Mexico protectorate status. A few months before Danville, on February 6, his proposal to the U.S. Senate for a protectorate over Mexico and Central America had met defeat by a 33–16 vote. He had consequently watered down the proposal to just Mexico in a subsequent Senate speech on April 20. It was this latter idea that he sought to keep alive even as he ran for governor of Texas.

Lest Houston's idea seem preposterous, consider the condition of socioeconomic disrepair then encroaching upon Mexico. Just thirteen months after his Danville speech, in December 1859, Sam Houston would become governor for a second time. During that same month, in desperation, Mexico would offer the United States authority approaching that of a protector.

To the accompaniment of U.S. troops on the scene, the proposed McClane-Ocampo Treaty proffered the United States perpetual rights of transit across the Mexican Isthmus of Tehuantepec. It was politics of the Civil War—not demands of Mexico—that would doom the treaty. To the Mexicans, fear of foreign encroachment from Europe left the United States as the lesser evil.

As governor from December 1859 until he was deposed for his pro-Union views in March 1861, Sam Houston honed his strategy. His plan came close to activation as U.S. troops were ordered temporarily to the Mexican border in March 1860. Indeed, even as he was making the decision that aborted his governorship the next year, there were men-at-arms ready to follow him into Mexico; by then, however, Houston deemed the window of opportunity closed.

Historian Walter Prescott Webb, among others, believes that Houston's motives were laudable, centered as they were on bringing Americans, north

Sam Houston's gravesite in Oakwood Cemetery, Huntsville, Texas. On the marker is engraved the immortal words of Andrew Jackson: "The World will take care of Houston's fame." *Courtesy of Robin Montgomery.*

and south, together via the common goal of generating stability in Mexico—as an alternative to engaging each other in civil war.

With visions of this grand project, Sam Houston dazzled the gathering at Danville in September 1858. Could the United States' intersectional war have been delayed a while longer, what a difference the intriguing message from Danville might have made. On July 26, 1863, Sam Houston died in Huntsville; his last words were "Texas, Texas, Margaret."

It was after Houston's death that Joshua made the trip to Independence, where Margaret resided at the time. It was then that he made the dramatic offer of his savings, only to receive the request from her to use the funds for educating his family.

JOSHUA FACES FREEDOM

The news that slaves were free came from General Gordon Granger in Galveston on June 19, 1865, and spread like wildfire across Texas, well before General E.M. Gregory delivered it officially at Huntsville's First Methodist Church. All sides were in shock and disarray: the planters because they had crops in the field with their slaves leaving, and the former slaves who, after the initial thanksgiving, faced the hard fact that they were left to their own devices in a world for which most were unprepared.

Included among further problems were the following: Land in Texas was nearly worthless, as was the Confederate currency; transportation was disrupted; former slaves were looking for lost family members, while orphans were running the streets; hunger was rampant, adding to growing health problems; and rapes, murders and beatings were a daily affair, even to the point of some freed men and women being resubjected to bondage.

JOSHUA'S THREE ADVANTAGES

In the face of this carnage, Joshua was more fortunate than most. He had three key factors in his favor: He could read and write, most of the key people in town and surrounding areas knew him and he had taken the name of Houston. It was the Christian-educated among the freed slaves who took the early lead in bringing sustenance and comfort to their fellows. It was mainly to this cadre that the sympathetic among the whites offered their support, and it was largely white teachers from the North who sought positions in the church, where most educational endeavors occurred.

With his head start, Joshua purchased land just north of the courthouse from Micaiah Clark Rogers, first mayor of Huntsville. This set a tone that fortunate African Americans followed to make the area into a community, which they called Rogersville. Here Joshua lived a quality life until his passing in 1902, having served as the first African American to receive a political position in Huntsville, that of alderman, to be followed by election as a county commissioner. Meanwhile, his influence was pervasive in promoting upward mobility to his race and cultural togetherness.

AN EXAMPLE OF OUR PROJECTED APPROACH TO HISTORICAL ANALYSIS

Let's engage an example of our suggested approach to the study of Texas and U.S. history, featuring Martin Luther King Jr. and Sam Houston.

Sam Houston, the liberator of Texas at the Battle of San Jacinto on April 21, 1836, went on to serve as the first president of the Republic of Texas, while later serving Texas in the U.S. Senate when Texas became a state. While possessor of a glittering political and military career—for example, he was the only person to be governor of two states, Tennessee and Texas—he considered his short career as a teacher in a one-room schoolhouse in Maryville, Tennessee, to be the most rewarding time in his life. Sam Houston understood the importance of depicting a true history as foundational to a sociopolitical culture.

As we've seen, this noble man lived much of his later life in Huntsville, Texas, in our Cradle Road area; his tomb in that city is a national landmark. Sam Houston epitomized conciliatory features, similar to those of Martin Luther King Jr.

Delineating those features is the subject of the following addendum.

POLITICALLY INCORRECT AS CORRECT: SAM HOUSTON AND MARTIN LUTHER KING JR.

The lives of Martin Luther King Jr. and Sam Houston provide a model for bringing some sense of unity out of the divisiveness that characterizes political correctness in our time. Fundamental to that divisiveness is the concept of cultural determinism, which holds that the subculture into which one is drawn at a formative age becomes the pivotal and ultimate determiner of one's values or standards of judgment. Subcultures are essentially genetically based, tied to race, which augments the separateness.

Reinforcing divisiveness is the concept of cultural appropriation. This is especially apparent in terms of the Black versus the white race. The tendency here is to label politically incorrect or racist any action by a member of the white race centered on displaying, or behaving in a manner associated with, Black culture, divorced from a "proper context" reflecting Black culture.

Stemming from these divisive premises, the greatest sin in pluralism lies in surrender to cultural assimilation, the merging of a subculture into the cultural mainstream, thereby diminishing the subculture's uniqueness. Tempering the presumed ill effects of cultural assimilation is acculturation. While bringing the representative of a subculture into the mainstream, acculturation allows for retention of a basic obeisance to one's native subculture.

It is against the background of acculturation so defined that Martin Luther King Jr. and Sam Houston become models of cultural integration in an era held captive by pluralist political correctness. Each of these men expressed the embrace of the dominant, assimilated U.S. culture as the goal of society generally, while continuing to pay respect to a subculture with which they identified. Witness Sam Houston's playing a pivotal role in the mainstream while also wearing apparel reflective of the Native American subculture, a habit finding sociopolitical legitimacy in his having spent quality time with Native Americans.

Reflecting aspects of acculturation, then, both King and Houston meet the test of political correctness. However, both, at the same time, challenged political correctness in the context of seeing each individual as equally significant, apart from and regardless of one's subcultural and biological roots.

This transformational act of political incorrectness marks the path to releasing the individual from the narrowly based groupthink of cultural determinism to embrace identity with the founding documents of our country's political and social institutions, common to all.

Reinforcing commonality, both Sam Houston and Martin Luther King Jr. were nationalists. In his "I Have a Dream" speech, King called for a coming together of heirs of slaves and slave masters to join in singing the refrain of "America (My Country, 'Tis of Thee)."

Then there was Sam Houston, who, as governor of Texas, willingly surrendered his high office as the price for refusing to sign Texas into the Confederacy due to his loyalty to the nation as a whole. Furthermore, Sam Houston freed his slaves prematurely, an act whose mark on later history was significant. As we've seen, Joshua Houston, slave of Houston's wife, Margaret, sought to give her his life savings on Sam Houston's death, an offer that she refused, urging him instead to use the money to educate his progeny. This Joshua did, while his son, Samuel Walker Houston, following Sam Houston as a model, became both a state and nationally recognized figure in education and racial conciliation.

Featuring broad-based nationalism while yet respecting subcultural roots, Sam Houston and Martin Luther King Jr. are models for a unity of substance even within a pluralist framework. Sam Houston, hero of San Jacinto, and Martin Luther King Jr., the great visionary of racial unity, are examples worthy of emulation in a revitalized approach to Texas and U.S. history.

SONGS OF THE CRADLE ROAD

"CRADLE OF TEXAS ROAD"

Robin Montgomery, October 26, 2012

There is a road in Texas, unique to that fine state.
It marks a path of greatness, of that there's no mistake.
It's the work of many cultures, and nations great and small.
Together they made Texas, the answer to freedom's call.

Here we learn that Colonel Travis drew a line in Alamo sand,
and of a mighty marshal, the fastest in the land.
And here a French explorer set Spain's head to spin,
to name the new land *Tejas*, an Indian word for friend.

Chorus:
It's the Cradle of Texas Road, where legends come alive,
legends that were born there, then spread far and wide.
From the first Native Americans, and many battle scars,
it holds the key to the names of Texas, from Spain to stars and bars.

From the banks of River Brazos, whose name means Arms of God,
To near the River Trinity, where Texas heroes trod,
Old San Antonio, the road of its northern bounds,
harbors dreams of glorious Texas and battles of renown.

Repeat chorus

The Cradle of Texas Is a Road of Togetherness
"They Celebrated Togetherness"

Robin Montgomery, January 12, 2011

The first Republic of Texas was an offshoot of Miguel Hidalgo, the Father of Mexico, kicking off the Mexican Revolution of September 16, 1810. The first Republic was initially announced in the vicinity of the northeast corner of original Montgomery County, part of our Cradle of Texas Road, in October 1812.

Times were rough down in Mexico,
the Spanish held the land, wouldn't let go.
But one man, named Gutiérrez de Lara,
turned to the north like there was no tomorrow.
Like a man possessed, he headed for the United States.
That country held the key to Mexico's fate.

It was 1813 when de Lara returned,
but he had with him men who for freedom yearned.
Men who had fought, to save their land,
now here in Mexico would make a stand.
They stopped in San Antonio, there they put up a flag,
defeated the Spanish, so they could brag.

It was the Green Flag Republic, the first free state in the land.
A free state in Spanish Texas, built with Mexican and Anglo hands.
They wrote the first constitution of Texas, names signed with *X*'s.
Then in the wilderness, they celebrated togetherness.

Juntos estamos, estamos juntos hasta el fin
Trabajando y jugando en paz, nuestro sueño, our dream.

Addendum II

"Who Were the Bidai?"

Robin Montgomery, April 7, 2021

Bidai Indians claimed to be the original Indians of Texas and therefore the leaders of Texas. By the time of the Anglo influx, their powers had been greatly eclipsed, due in large part to a great natural calamity while the majority were living in Bucareli, in the northeastern sector of the original Montgomery County. They continued, however, to have a presence and impact, through cunning, over the whole region of our Cradle of Texas Road. The Caddo themselves claimed that the Bidai built what are known as the Great Caddo Mounds. The main strength of the Bidai came through the reputation of their shaman, who, other tribes believed, could turn into owls and cast spells, for good or ill. One of their exotic practices lay in head-flattening at birth.

Who were the Bidai? Many do not know.
The strongest tribe in Texas, a long time ago.
Their wisdom was profound, they built the huge Caddo Mounds.
The Bidai Tribe in Texas, on hallowed ground.

Their medicine men were powerful, shaman oh so strong,
turning themselves into owls, scaring those who might do wrong.
With the Bidai in control, things were good, for young and old.
The Bidai Tribe in Texas, noble and bold.

Chorus:
Over all of Texas was their reign,
from the forest to the plains, they made their claim.
But they longed to be between the Brazos and the Trinity.
On the Cradle of Texas Road, happy and free.

"LA SALLE, THE FOUNDATION"

Robin Montgomery, April 7, 2021

La Salle was a French explorer who, upon discovering the route to the mouth of the Mississippi, claimed all lands drained by that great river for France. He then returned to France, secured four ships and returned, intending to set up a business in the area. Unfortunately, he bypassed the great river and landed at Matagorda Bay, along the way eventually losing control of all his ships. By marching to the Rio Grande, he set the stage for Thomas Jefferson to make his claim that the Louisiana Purchase made the Rio Grande the border of Texas, laying a basis for the Mexican-American War of 1846–48. As related earlier, his death near Navasota gave vent to actions resulting in the expedition of Alonso de León and Father Massanet to establish San Francisco de las Tejas, resulting in the name of Texas. On one of his trips searching for the Mississippi, he passed through present Dacus, perhaps marking the first encounter of Europeans with the Bidai.

La Salle, the man, the dream. Impact on history, supreme.
He set the stage, profound, on which the Cradle of Texas Road was found.
Jefferson and Houston, to name a few on which his impact came through.
René-Robert Cavelier, Sieur de la Salle, echoes linger for one and all.

Into the Texas coast he came, lost but pursuing his fame.
Marching to the Rio Grande was key to marking his place in history.
La Salle, adventurer supreme, foundation of the Cradle of Texas Dream.

"THE LAD FROM MARYVILLE"

Robin Montgomery, June 2015

Sam Houston's boyhood home was in Maryville, Tennessee, where there is a statue of the young Sam Houston. We participated in its dedication with a tour of people from our area. Robin's part was to perform this song. It was from Maryville that the young Sam Houston left to live for a time with the Cherokee Indians at Hiwassee Island, where he met an Indian maiden who would much later become his second wife, before he married Margaret Lea. It was also from Maryville that he left to join Andrew Jackson and company at the Battle of Horseshoe Bend. Reacting to criticism as he left Maryville, Houston exclaimed, "You shall hear of me!" Also at Maryville, for a while, the young Sam Houston taught school in a one-room schoolhouse. He said this was the most rewarding experience of his life.

On the grand Hiwassee Island, in the River Tennessee,
lived some Native Americans, of the tribe of Cherokee.

From nearby Maryville, to join this community,
came young Sam Houston, seeking liberty.

There he met the fair Diana, niece of John Jolly.
She became the guiding star of Sam's destiny.

*Man of many nations, Sam set a people free,
and they gave the name of Texas to a brand new country.*

The grand Hiwassee Island, enchanted land of thrills.
It sparked the imagination of the lad from Maryville.

The lad fought at Horseshoe Bend, allied to the Cherokee,
He went to war with confidence, saying, "You shall hear of me!"

*A man of many nations, Sam set a people free,
And they gave the name of Texas to a brand new country.*

"Travis Drew a Line"

Robin Montgomery, April 7, 2021

On March 3, 1836, William B. Travis, in command at the Alamo, called his forces together and drew a line in the sand with his sword. He then related their situation: with a superior force, Santa Anna had them surrounded, with no chance of survival. He then offered them a chance for freedom, saying if any chose to leave, this was the moment. History recorded that all crossed the line, with none choosing to stay. However, years later, William Zuber wrote that one man did cross, Moses Rose, and came to his father and mother's home. The song below depicts this story.

In 1836 came Travis, the man, to draw a line in the Alamo sand.
"Santa Anna," he said with a cry, "has us surrounded, we all shall die.
"If you cross this line, the die is cast. We'll fight Santa Anna to the very last."

Every man that day crossed that line. Or so it appeared at that time.
But one man, we later would know, did not cross; he wanted to go.
He set his route; to Shiro he came.
The "Imposter of the Alamo" would be his name.

Chorus:
They called him Moses Rose, honored veteran, but freedom he chose.
As a man, Moses Rose was brave. It might've been different had he stayed.
It seems forever we'll never know why Moses Rose left the Alamo.

"Joshua Hadley"

Robin Montgomery, October 1, 2021

Joshua Hadley was alcalde of Washington Municipality, incorporating all or part of present Washington, Brazos, Burleson and Lee Counties west of the Brazos and Montgomery, Walker, Grimes, San Jacinto, Madison and Waller on the east side. Remains of Hadley's fort and homesite are yet in Roans Prairie.

Josh Hadley and his family lived on Hadley's Prairie,
and a fort on his place kept his neighbors safe.
When in danger, from miles around they came.
Josh Hadley treated everyone the same.

In eighteen thirty-five, broader danger came alive.
A more secure site was found, for protection all around.
Off the Brazos, Washington was set to be
the capital of a huge territory.

Thus, a need for a leader, brave and strong,
who could help the people carry on.
Josh Hadley was that leader who came to be
the alcalde of Washington Municipality.

On both sides of the Brazos, broad was his reign,
but Joshua Hadley treated everyone the same.
A pioneer for all seasons, his story we have told,
of a mighty man of valor, on the Cradle of Texas Road.

"Flags of the Cradle Road"

Robin Montgomery, July 10, 2021

Sarah Dodson, buried near Bedias, and Charles Stewart of Montgomery designed similar Lone Star flags. The difference: one had vertical, the other horizontal, stripes.

In the lore of Texas history, flags spelled freedom.
From Revolution to Republic, proud they flew.
The Cradle of Texas Road featured two.

During the Revolution, Sarah Dodson was the key.
She sewed a flag for her husband's company.
In a blue strip was a lone star, colored white,
with *vertical* white and red colored stripes.

Charles Stewart's colors, in the Republic, were the same.
But white and red stripes were on a *horizontal* plane.
Stewart's flag still shines!
The official flag of Texas, for all time.

Dodson and Stewart are legends of our Road,
With gravesites here, both well-kept and mowed.
Sarah's in Bethel Cemetery,
while Stewart rests in Old Montgomery.

Giants in Texas history are these two.
We're proud to share their story with all of you.

INDEX

ABOUT THE AUTHORS

Robin Navarro Montgomery

Robin is a native of Conroe, Texas, and holds a PhD from the University of Oklahoma. His professional background includes a career as professor at Southwestern Oklahoma State University, along with four years as professor of international relations for a graduate program in Europe for U.S. military officers. He also served as vice president for academic affairs at Oxford Graduate School in Dayton, Tennessee (now Omega), and is a member of the Oxford Society of Scholars.

Robin Montgomery is making a presentation at the gravesite of Sam Houston, when he was chairman of the Walker County Historical Commission. *Courtesy of the* Huntsville Item.

Robin has published extensively in political science and local history, including professional articles, books and newspaper columns. His previous books include *Cuban Shadow Over Southern Cones: The Vietnam, African-American Connection*; *The History of Montgomery County, Texas* (two editions); *Cut 'n Shoot, Texas*; *Tortured Destiny: Lament of a Shaman Princess* (historical novel); *Historic Montgomery County*; *Indians and Pioneers of Original Montgomery County*; *March to Destiny: Cultural Legacy of Stephen F. Austin's Original Colony*; *Conroe: Transformation of the Miracle City*; *Mary McCoy: Country Music Legend*; with Joy Montgomery, *Navasota* ("Images of America" series, Arcadia

Publishing); *The Cradle of Texas Road*; *Sam Houston's Quest: The Cherokee and African-American Virtue Agenda*; with Roy Harris, *Roy Harris of Cut and Shoot: Backwards Battler*; and with Sondra Hernandez, Joy Montgomery and Larry Foerster, an Arcadia book on *Conroe*.

JOY RENEE MONTGOMERY

Joy Montgomery with image of Charles Stewart, first Texas secretary of state, in the background. *Courtesy of Heritage Museum of Montgomery County.*

Joy holds an MA in English and history from Sam Houston State University and a BA in German, including receipt of a certificate while in Germany as demonstration of official fluency. She has served in the Peace Corps in Kyrgyzstan and held teaching positions in that country, as well as in Germany and South Korea. Joy has worked in Washington, D.C., with Housing and Urban Development and with Oxford Graduate School in Dayton, Tennessee, and she has held the position of grant analyst for the state of Tennessee in Nashville. Her background further includes the position of executive director of the Heritage Museum of Montgomery County, Texas, and she served as a museum specialist at Sequoyah Birthplace Museum in Tennessee. Joy has also held the positions of secretary of the Tennessee Trail of Tears and administrative assistant in the United Nations' related work with Indigenous people. Her previous books, in association with Robin Montgomery, include *The Cradle of Texas Road*, *Sam Houston's Quest* and Arcadia books on *Navasota* and *Conroe*.

Joy Montgomery and her daughter, Katie Robin. *From personal family files. Courtesy of Joy Montgomery.*

Visit us at
www.historypress.com
....